A STRESS-FREE GUIDE TO FINANCIAL LITERACY FOR TEENS & YOUNG ADULTS

MASTER MONEY MANAGEMENT, AVOID COSTLY MISTAKES, INVEST LIKE A PRO, AND SECURE YOUR FINANCIAL FUTURE

MONEY MENTOR PUBLICATIONS

TABLE OF CONTENTS

GET YOUR FREE

INTERACTIVE BUDGET TRACKING
SPREADSHEET

SCAN FOR A FREE TEMPLATE

EASILY TRACK INCOME AND EXPENSES FOR 9 DIFFERENT CATEGORIES

MONEY MENTOR PUBLICATIONS

INTRODUCTION

Have you ever been hit with a sudden, "Wait, how am I supposed to do this?" feeling when trying to figure out how to manage your first paycheck, deciding whether to splurge on that new phone or save up for your first car? You're not alone. Most of us have stared at our bank statements in confusion, wishing we had a guide to decode all the financial mumbo jumbo. It feels like everyone else got a crash course in managing money while we're left scrambling to figure it out on our own. One of the most crucial lessons teens and young adults need is how to handle money wisely, yet our schools often leave us in the dark on this important subject.

That's exactly why this book exists. It's here to translate the complex language of finance into something you can understand and use. It's a guide from financial confusion to clarity and empowerment, written specifically for you, the teen or young adult stepping into the world of money management.

This isn't your typical finance book. We've tossed out the boring lectures and infused the pages with stories you'll actually want to read. Expect to see anecdotes that mirror your experiences and real-world examples that make sense. Why? Because learning about money doesn't have to be a snooze fest.

The goal here is simple: to make you financially literate in a world where digital banking, cryptocurrency, and the gig economy are becoming the norm. We're talking about real skills that will help you navigate your daily financial decisions and plan for a future where you're in charge.

Alarmingly, many teens and young adults are left out of the loop when it comes to financial education. Did you know that 75% of people your age feel clueless about managing their finances? This gap can lead to anxiety, unnecessary debt, and missed opportunities. It doesn't have to be this way.

You—the YouTube-watching, meme-sharing, TikTok-scrolling generation—are ready to change the narrative. You dream of financial independence, making smart investment choices, and avoiding the debt traps that snagged previous generations. This book is here to help you do just that.

We'll tackle everything from crafting a budget that fits your lifestyle to understanding how to start investing with just a little cash. We'll decode the mysteries of credit scores, explore ways to boost your earnings, and even dive into the basics of taxes.

We know what you might be thinking: "I don't have enough money to manage," or "Finance books are too dense." Hear us out. This book is crafted with your concerns in mind. It's tailored for beginners and packed with interactive tools that you can personalize. Most importantly, it's written in a style that speaks to you—not at you.

So, let's kick-start this journey together. By the end of this book, you will be equipped to make informed financial decisions and feel confident about securing a future where you call the financial shots. Ready to take control of your money? Let's get started.

CHAPTER 1

FINANCIAL FOUNDATIONS: BUILDING YOUR KNOWLEDGE FROM THE GROUND UP

The number one problem in today's generation and economy is the lack of financial literacy.

ALAN GREENSPAN

Getting ready to step out into the world on your own two feet for the first time is a rush—exciting, a bit scary, and undeniably liberating. It's like standing on the edge of a new world where every decision is yours, from what you eat for breakfast to how late you stay up. Among these newfound freedoms, one superpower stands above the rest: managing your money. Get this right, and you're in control; get it wrong, and you could be in for a turbulent ride that impacts your life for years to come. No pressure, right? Remember, knowledge is power! The more you know about how to handle your finances, the more freedom and security you will have in the future!

Let's discover what can happen when money management skills are neglected during your student years.

1.1 THE RISKS OF IGNORING FINANCIAL EDUCATION

1. Independence Delay - *Ethan's Epiphany*

During his senior year of high school, Ethan landed his first part-time job at a local café and relished the freedom that came with his first paycheck. Eager to enjoy his earnings, he splurged on a new gaming console and nights out with friends, overlooking his parents' advice to save. As graduation approached, Ethan dreamed of moving out and starting his independent life. However, when the time came to put down a deposit for an apartment, Ethan realized that he hadn't saved nearly enough to cover the initial expenses. Unable to afford the move, he had to delay his plans for independence and stay at home longer than he wanted, struggling to save up while watching his peers embark on their new lives. This frustrating setback taught Ethan the value of financial foresight and saving for major life steps.

2. Overwhelmed by Overdrafts - *Emily's Tale*

Emily was thrilled to start her college life and be independent. With her first bank account, she felt ready to handle her own finances. Excited by her new freedom, she splurged on dorm decorations, new clothes, and hanging out with friends. However, Emily didn't keep track of her spending. By the end of the first month, she faced multiple bank overdraft fees after exceeding her account balance. Each purchase pushed her deeper into the red, culminating in over $100 in bank fees. This harsh lesson taught Emily the importance of budgeting and monitoring her bank account regularly to avoid drowning in avoidable fees.

3. Credit Card Chaos - *Josh's Journey*

Josh received his first credit card with a $1,000 limit as he entered university. He viewed it as free money, using it to fund extravagant outings and electronics to enhance his college experience. Josh quickly maxed out his card without understanding the impact of high interest and minimum payments. When the bill arrived, he could only afford the minimum payment, not realizing that it barely covered the interest. This led to a ballooning balance and a plummeting credit score. It took Josh years to recover, learning the hard way that credit isn't an extension of income.

4. The Hidden Costs of Renting - *Lara's Lesson*

Lara signed her first apartment lease without reviewing the terms closely or understanding the full cost of living on her own. Excited to be independent, she overlooked expenses like utilities, internet, and renter's insurance, which were not included in the rent. Midway through the semester, Lara struggled to cover these additional costs, forcing her to skimp on essentials like food and heating. This experience taught her to review all lease and utility agreements meticulously and to plan a comprehensive budget that includes all living expenses, avoiding financial strains that can come from unexpected bills.

Stepping into independence doesn't have to mean stumbling through financial pitfalls. Arm yourself with the right know-how from this guide, and you're set to sail smoothly over the hurdles that trip up the unprepared. Dive into these pages, and you'll gather golden nuggets of wisdom that will have you managing your money like a boss. Picture a life where financial fumbles don't darken your days or burden your future. By adopting good money habits now, you'll dodge the stress and anxiety that plague many, basking in freedom and choice that others can only envy. Every smart save, wise spend, and insightful investment steers your present, secures your independence, and carves out a thriving future exactly as you envision it.

Imagine starting your own business or diving into the world of real estate with confidence. These aren't just dreams—they're entirely achievable realities with a solid financial foundation laid down early. Embrace these skills now, and not only will you easily navigate life's monetary challenges, but you'll also stand miles ahead of your peers. While they're still wrestling with the basics, you'll be mastering the art of making your money work for you.

1.2 UNLOCKING THE POWER OF FINANCIAL LITERACY

Financial literacy isn't just about numbers; it's about gaining control over your financial life. It means knowing how to budget so you don't end up broke before payday, saving so you have a cushion for emergencies, and investing wisely to grow your wealth. It's also about managing debt without getting buried and understanding how credit works so you don't get hit with high interest rates. Being financially literate helps you make smart choices with your money, like whether to splurge or to save for future goals. It's about reading financial statements without getting lost, grasping how interest rates can affect you, and keeping a good credit score. In short, it's about setting yourself up for financial stability, avoiding unnecessary debt, and building wealth over time.

Mellody Hobson, Chairperson of Starbucks, said it best:

If you understand how money can work for you and against you, you can make better decisions. Financial literacy is not about wealth but about understanding money regardless of the amount. It's about how you treat it and how you maximize opportunities.

Let's look at some examples of how learning good money skills now will help you get ahead of the curve.

1. Jameson's Smart Savings

Jameson, a high school senior, started saving a portion of his allowance and part-time job earnings early on. He opened a high-yield savings account and set up automatic transfers to ensure he consistently saved money. By the time he graduated, Jameson had saved enough to cover his first year of college expenses, reducing his reliance on student loans and giving him a financial head start.

2. Jenna's Budgeting Success

Jenna, a college freshman, created a budget as soon as she started receiving her scholarship funds and part-time job earnings. She used budgeting apps to track her spending, ensuring she lived within her means. By avoiding unnecessary expenses and prioritizing her needs, Jenna saved a significant amount of money each month, which she later used to study abroad without financial stress.

3. AJ's Investment Journey

AJ, a 19-year-old college student, took a personal finance course in high school that sparked his interest in investing. He started small by investing in low-cost index funds and learning about the stock market through books and online resources. By regularly contributing to his investment portfolio and taking advantage of compound interest, AJ saw steady growth in his investments, setting himself up for long-term financial success.

4. Korinne's Entrepreneurial Spirit

Korinne, a teenager passionate about baking, turned her hobby into a small business. She carefully managed her earnings, reinvesting in her business and saving a portion of her profits. By keeping track of her expenses and setting financial goals, Korinne expanded her business and saved enough to fund her college education without taking on debt.

Dedicating time to learning personal finance is one of the best investments you can make. It puts you in control of your future, reduces money-related stress, and opens doors to financial independence. The good news is that you don't need to make a lot of money to achieve financial independence; it's not about how much you earn but how you manage what you have. Many believe a high salary guarantees financial security, but that's not always the case. There are countless examples of millionaires who have worked blue-collar jobs their entire lives, diligently saving and investing wisely.

On the other hand, some doctors and other professionals earning substantial incomes find themselves broke due to poor financial habits and excessive spending. Financial independence hinges on living within your means, budgeting effectively, saving consistently, and making smart investments. By adopting these practices, you can build wealth and achieve financial stability regardless of income level. So, don't wait—start building your financial knowledge today and enjoy the benefits for years to come.

1.3 NAVIGATING YOUR BANK ACCOUNT: WHAT ALL THE TERMS MEAN

If you don't already have your own bank account, the time has come to get one. There are a lot of banks and credit unions to choose from, so here are a few things to consider when opening that first account:

Fees and Charges

- **Monthly Maintenance Fees**: Look for accounts with no or low monthly fees. Many banks offer free student checking accounts or accounts with fee waivers if certain conditions are met, such as maintaining a minimum balance or setting up direct deposit.
- **ATM Fees**: Consider the availability of ATMs and whether the bank charges fees for using out-of-network ATMs. Some banks offer reimbursements for these fees.
- **Overdraft Fees**: Check the bank's overdraft policy and associated fees. Some banks offer overdraft protection plans that link to a savings account to cover transactions.

Account Features

- **Interest Rates**: Compare the interest rates offered on savings accounts, checking accounts, and certificates of deposit (CDs). Higher interest rates can help your money grow faster.
- **Mobile and Online Banking**: Ensure the bank provides robust online and mobile banking services. Features to look for include mobile check deposit, bill pay, and account alerts.
- **Minimum Balance Requirements**: Some accounts require a minimum balance to avoid fees or to earn interest. Make sure these requirements align with your financial situation.

Accessibility and Convenience

- **Branch Locations**: If you prefer in-person banking services, consider the convenience of branch locations.

Some online banks have limited or no physical branches but may offer other benefits.

- **Customer Service**: Research the bank's reputation for customer service. Look for reviews and ratings to see how current customers feel about their experiences.
- **Ease of Account Opening**: Check the process for opening an account. Some banks offer entirely online account opening processes, which can be more convenient.

Security and Trust

- **FDIC/NCUA Insurance**: Ensure the bank or credit union is insured by the FDIC (Federal Deposit Insurance Corporation) or the NCUA (National Credit Union Administration). This insurance protects your deposits up to $250,000.
- **Security Features**: Look for security features, such as two-factor authentication, fraud alerts, and secure login processes, to protect your account information.

Credit Union vs. Bank

- **Credit Unions**: These often offer lower fees and better interest rates on loans and savings accounts because they are non-profit institutions owned by their members. However, membership may be restricted to certain groups.
- **Banks**: These typically offer more products and services, including a wider range of loans, credit cards, and investment services. They also tend to have more branch locations and ATMs.

Special Programs and Benefits

- **Student Accounts**: Many banks offer special accounts designed for students, which may include perks, such as waived fees or discounts on loans.
- **Rewards Programs**: Some banks offer rewards programs for using their debit or credit cards, which can provide cash back, points, or other incentives.

If you already have your account, let's be honest: the first time you opened it, it may have felt a bit like venturing into a bizarre new universe where everything seemed overly complicated. You were probably handed a stack of paperwork thicker than your favorite diner's menu, with a lot of unfamiliar terms and options. Well, it's time to sort all that out. From checking accounts that feel like your financial "checking in" points to savings accounts that are more like your money's cozy long-term home, understanding these can make you feel less like you're reading a foreign language and more like you're taking charge of your cash.

Account Types: More Than Just Places to Stash Your Cash

First are *Checking Accounts*. These are your everyday financial tool-boxes. They're perfect for daily transactions, like getting that burrito from the food truck or paying your electric bill. They usually come with a debit card, which might become your new best friend for easy access to your funds. While they're convenient for frequent use, they're not meant to grow your wealth.

Switch gears to *Savings Accounts*, and you're entering a different vibe. Here's where your money sits back, relaxes, and slowly grows through something magical called interest, the money the bank pays you to keep your money there. It's similar to planting and watching a tree grow over the years. You won't use a savings account for daily expenses; rather, it's perfect for your long-term goals, like that summer road trip, your own car, or perhaps eventually, a down payment on your first condo.

There are also hybrids and specialties: ***Money Market Accounts*** and ***Certificates of Deposit (CDs)***. Money market accounts are like the cool cousins of the regular savings account, typically offering higher interest rates in return for higher balance requirements. CDs? Think of them as time capsules for your cash. You lock away your money at a fixed interest rate for a set period, and—Bam!—more money at the end of the term.

Understanding Fees: Dodge Those Sneaky Charges

Now, on to something less fun—bank fees. Have you ever been slapped with a fee for withdrawing your own money from an ATM that wasn't affiliated with your bank? Maybe you've felt the sting of an overdraft fee when you miscalculated and spent more than what was in your account. These fees sneak up on you, but there are ways to outsmart them. For ATMs, it's about knowing where your bank's machines are located or getting an account that offers ATM fee rebates. Overdraft fees? Opt into alerts that notify you when you're close to zero or link your checking to your savings for automatic coverage. You can discuss available options when you open your bank account, or if it's already up and running, visit your bank and ask them about all of the features they have to help you avoid unnecessary fees. Your goal is never to pay a dime in bank fees, and it is 100% possible with a little care and attention.

Banking Services: Your Financial Swiss Army Knife

Today's online banking features are all about convenience and efficiency. Most banks now offer features like automatic transfers, which you can set up to funnel money into your savings account or to pay bills automatically. It's like setting a cruise control for your financial obligations; once you set it, you can sit back and focus on other things.

Alerts are another game changer. Get a text or email when your balance dips below a certain amount or when a large transaction goes through. Since you'll be the first to know if something's up with your accounts, you have peace of mind. Many banks also offer spending insights, showing you pie charts or bar graphs of your monthly spending divided into categories. It's a quick and visual way to get a sense of where your money is going without digging through all your statements.

Safety and Security: Protecting Your Treasure

Finally, let's talk about safety. In an age when data breaches seem as common as the latest TikTok that just went viral, knowing how to protect your bank account is crucial. First rule? Create strong, unique passwords for your online banking accounts. Think less "123456" and more "$ecureP@ssw0rd!2025." Also, always log out completely after accessing banking info on public or shared comput-ers. Your bank plays defense with measures like encryption and fraud monitoring. However, staying informed about the latest security, like two-factor authentication, adds an extra layer of armor around your finances.

We started this chapter by highlighting the significance of financial literacy in establishing a solid foundation for managing personal finances and avoiding common pitfalls. Next, we'll dive into the intricacies of budgeting, but before that, here's a handy checklist to guide you through setting up your bank account effectively:

ACTION STEPS FOR SETTING UP YOUR BANK ACCOUNT:

1. Research Banks and Credit Unions:

- Compare fees and charges.
- Evaluate account features like interest rates and mobile banking.
- Consider accessibility and convenience.

2. Understand Account Types:

- Know the differences among checking, savings, money market accounts, and CDs.

3. Review Fees:

- Look for accounts with no or low monthly maintenance fees.
- Be aware of ATM and overdraft fees, and explore options for overdraft protection.

4. Examine Account Features:

- Be sure that there are robust online and mobile banking services.
- Verify minimum balance requirements and other requirements.

5. Evaluate Security:

- Ensure that the bank is insured by FDIC or NCUA.
- Look for strong security features like two-factor authentication.

6. Explore Special Programs:

- Investigate student accounts and rewards programs.

CHAPTER 2
BUDGETING BASICS

A Budget is telling your money where to go instead of wondering where it went.

DAVE RAMSEY

Imagine you're at your favorite restaurant with friends, menu in hand. Do you splurge on that overpriced but oh-so-tempting gourmet entrée, or do you stick with the more budget-friendly option? Life is full of these little choices when what you decide in the moment can impact your wallet in bigger ways than you might think. That's where a solid budget comes into play—not as a buzzkill to all your fun, but as a financial GPS guiding you through daily decisions and beyond. Let's break down the art of budgeting.

2.1 CRAFTING YOUR FIRST BUDGET: A STEP-BY-STEP GUIDE

Setting Financial Goals: A Compass for Your Cash

Setting financial goals is like picking a destination before you start driving; it's essential. Without a destination, you might go in circles or, even worse, get lost in the middle of nowhere. Financial goals work the same way. They give your money a purpose and keep you motivated, whether it's saving up for a concert ticket, managing car payments, or making your first investments.

Start by distinguishing between short-term and long-term goals. Short-term goals might include saving for a new laptop or funding a weekend road trip. These are typically goals you can achieve within a year. Long-term goals require more time and commitment, like saving for a car or education. Both types of goals are important; they just play different roles in your financial strategy. By identifying these, you're creating a blueprint that aligns your financial habits with your personal aspirations, making each dollar work toward something meaningful.

Tracking Income and Expenses: Your Financial Mirror

Now, let's get into the nitty-gritty—tracking your income and expenses. You need a clear picture of what comes in and what goes out. Start by listing all your sources of income, including that part-time job and any side hustles. Then, dive into your expenses. This means all of them—rent, food, subscriptions, gas/bus money—each penny needs to be accounted for.

This might sound tedious, and you might be tempted to estimate, but resist the urge. Estimations can lead to financial blind spots. Use tools like banking apps, spreadsheets, or even good old pen and paper to keep track. The good news is that you don't have to reinvent the wheel when it comes to finding a free downloadable interactive budget spreadsheet that will work for you. A simple Google search for "Free Google Sheets budget template" or "Free Excel budget templates" will give you many options to choose from.

You can also download our free budget tracking spreadsheet here: https://bit.ly/3yXeT0w

The most important thing is to take action and do it! It will help you understand your spending behaviors so you can adjust them to align with your financial goals.

In an effort to keep it real, we need to let you know that life is more expensive than you think it will be. Inflation over the last few years is giving everyone a bit of sticker shock when it comes to buying the essentials.

If you are still living at home, your budget will look different from someone who is already living on their own. Here's a list of potential expenses you need to prepare for as you move on to the next phase of your life:

Upfront Costs

- **Security Deposit**: Typically, landlords require one to two months' rent to cover potential damages. You may be able to get some or all of this back when you move out.
- **First and Last Month's Rent**: Many landlords require both upfront.
- **Application Fees**: There may also be costs for background and credit checks.

- **Moving Costs**: You may need to rent a moving truck and/or buy packing supplies.
- **Utility Deposits**: Deposits are used to set up services like electricity, gas, water, and internet.

Recurring Monthly Expenses

- **Rent**: The primary expense varies widely by location.
- **Utilities**: Read your lease carefully to see what is and isn't included, such as electricity, gas, water, sewer, and trash removal.
- **Internet and Cable**: This includes connectivity, data, and entertainment costs.
- **Renter's Insurance**: This provides coverage for personal belongings and liability.
- **Groceries**: Obviously, this includes food and household supplies.
- **Transportation**: You may have car payments, insurance, gas, and vehicle maintenance, or you may have public transportation costs.

Household Essentials

- **Furniture**: Bed, couch, tables, chairs, and other essential furniture
- **Kitchen Supplies**: Pots, pans, utensils, dishes, and small appliances
- **Cleaning Supplies**: Vacuum, mop, cleaning products, and other essentials
- **Bathroom Supplies**: Towels, shower curtains, toiletries, and cleaning items
- **Bedding**: Sheets, pillows, blankets, and mattress protectors

Additional Expenses

- **Laundry**: Costs for in-unit laundry or using laundromats
- **Personal Care Items**: Shampoo, soap, toothpaste, and other personal hygiene products
- **Entertainment and Dining Out**: Budgeted costs for social activities and eating out
- **Health Insurance**: Premiums if not covered under a parent's plan or provided by your employer
- **Emergency Fund**: Savings for unexpected expenses like medical emergencies or car repairs
- **Subscription Services**: Streaming services, magazines, gym memberships, etc.

Miscellaneous

- **Repairs and Maintenance**: Minor repairs and maintenance not covered by the landlord
- **Decor**: Items to personalize your space, like artwork, plants, and rugs
- **Storage**: Costs for renting additional storage space if needed

Remember to plan for all the little things you've never had to think about before, like toilet tissue, dishwashing detergent, and garbage bags. They add up quickly and can affect your overall budget.

Allocating Funds: Divide and Conquer

With a clear understanding of your income and expenses, it's time to allocate your funds. Think of your money as a pie you can slice in various ways. Some slices might be bigger, like rent or tuition, while others might be smaller, like entertainment or dining out. Here's the trick: prioritize your essentials first—housing, food, transportation, and necessary bills. The slice that's left can be divided among your savings and a few extras that you want.

A practical approach here is the 50/30/20 rule, in which 50% of your income goes to needs, 30% to wants, and 20% to savings. Adjust these percentages based on what best fits your situation. Maybe you're in a tight spot, and it will be more like 70/20/10. It's okay. The goal is to create a balance that supports stability but still allows room for enjoyment.

Adjusting Your Budget: Staying Agile

Your first budget won't be perfect. It's a living document that evolves. Regular check-ins are key. Sit down at least monthly to review how well your budget works. Are you consistently over-spending in one area? Do you have a little more wiggle room than expected? Adjustments might be necessary, and that's perfectly fine.

Life throws curveballs—unexpected expenses like a phone screen repair or a traffic ticket. Your budget needs to be flexible enough to accommodate these without derailing your financial goals.

Budget Adjustment Checklist

To help you stay on top of your budget adjustments, here's a handy checklist:

1. **Review your financial goals:** Are they still relevant? Have your priorities shifted?
2. **Analyze your spending:** Look for patterns or areas where you consistently overspend.
3. **Adjust your allocations:** Modify your budget slices to better fit your current needs.

4. **Plan for surprises:** Always have a small buffer for unexpected expenses.

Regular use of this checklist can turn a once-daunting task into a quick and simple routine, ensuring your budget remains an effective tool for financial success.

Saving vs. Splurging: Balancing Act of the Century

Here's the million-dollar question: how do you decide when to save and when to splurge? Imagine you're a chef creating a dish, trying to balance flavors perfectly. Just as you carefully measure each ingredient to create harmony, you'll want to find the right balance in your finances, too.

Start with understanding the value of what you're buying. Does it add to your life in a meaningful way, or is it just going to collect dust?

An easy trick is to calculate the cost per use. For instance, that expensive pair of boots might seem like a splurge, but if you wear them every day this winter, the cost per wear makes them a bargain compared to a cheap pair that falls apart after a few uses.

Another approach is to calculate how many hours you will have to work to pay for a particular thing, which also gives you some perspective and helps you to decide if it is really worth it.

Another tactic is to set waiting periods for large purchases. Give yourself a set time, maybe a week or two, before pulling the trigger on anything that costs more than a set amount. This cooling-off period can save you from impulse buys you might regret later. If you still want it just as much after the wait, and if it fits within your budget without derailing your savings goals, it's likely a worthwhile purchase.

Avoid overspending. Recognizing your triggers to overspend is like tuning into your personal frequency. Start by identifying what prompts you to reach for your wallet. Is it a stressful shift at work, a scroll through social media, or perhaps an "on-sale" sign that you can't resist? Once you know your triggers, you can set up guardrails. For example, avoid browsing online stores when you're bored or stressed. Instead, distract yourself with a hobby or chat with a friend.

Making a game out of frugal living can be both fun and rewarding. Challenge yourself to find treasures at garage sales, thrift stores, and bargain bins. You'd be amazed at what people are willing to part with for a fraction of the original price. Repurposing items is another creative way to save. Turn an old ladder into a bookshelf, or use mason jars as stylish storage. The thrill of the hunt and the satisfaction of a good deal can make thrifty living feel like an exciting adventure rather than a chore.

2.2 THE IMPACT OF SOCIAL MEDIA ON SPENDING HABITS

Social media significantly impacts the buying habits of teens and young adults by creating a constant stream of targeted advertisements and influencer endorsements that can be hard to resist. Platforms like Instagram, TikTok, and Snapchat are designed to keep users engaged, often showcasing trendy products and lifestyle images that promote a desire by users to emulate what they see. The ease of in-app shopping and the instant gratification of making a purchase with just a few clicks further fuel impulsive buying. Additionally, social media often blurs the line between genuine recommendations and paid promotions, making it challenging for users to distinguish between them. This constant exposure can lead to increased spending, often on nonessential items, and can contribute to financial strain and the development of poor money management habits.

The mechanics of this influence go beyond direct advertising. These platforms can also exacerbate social comparison, the insidious thief of joy. Seeing peers and influencers living what appears to be a higher standard of life can spark an internal desire to match or exceed that standard. You might find yourself splurging on brands tagged by influencers, booking a vacation to the "Insta-famous" beach you've seen all over your feed, or hunting down the dining set that perfectly matches the one in that viral Pinterest post. Social media platforms are designed to be addictive—the more time you spend on them, the more opportunities they have to learn what makes you tick and then tailor ads that tap directly into your desires.

Building Digital Resilience: Crafting Your Shield Against Consumerist Culture

It's possible to conquer the urge to impulse buy on social media by implementing a few mindful strategies. Start by pruning out influencers and brands that trigger your spending impulses or make you feel inadequate. Replace them with content that enriches your life and aligns with your values, like pages focused on budget travel, DIY home decor, or thrift fashion. This doesn't mean you can't follow any luxury brands or influencers, but it helps create a balance that keeps you grounded rather than always reaching for your wallet.

Additionally, become a savvy observer. Start recognizing targeted ads —those sneaky sales pitches that pop up after you've just searched for a product or talked about it near your smartphone. Most social media platforms offer options to control the ads you see, so take advantage of those settings to reduce the onslaught of temptation. It's also helpful to remind yourself that what you're seeing is often a highlight reel, not everyday reality. Those perfect moments captured on Instagram are just that—moments. They don't represent the full picture of anyone's life, including the debts or sacrifices made for that snapshot-worthy scene.

FOMO and Managing It: Turning Fear into Freedom

FOMO, or the Fear of Missing Out, is the pulse that often drives social media's influence on spending. It's the fear that everyone else is having a better time, owning better things, or living a better life—and it can lead to impulsive spending as you try to buy your way into the club of perceived happiness. Combatting FOMO starts with turning inward. Reflect on what truly brings you joy and satisfaction beyond the fleeting thrill of a purchase. Is it spending time with loved ones, pursuing a hobby, or maybe just the peace that comes with having no debt?

When you feel the tug of FOMO, pause and assess your motives. Are you considering a purchase because it genuinely aligns with your goals, or are you trying to fill a void that social media has magnified? Sometimes, the best way to manage FOMO is to log off and engage in real-life activities that reinforce your values and boost your mood. Engage in sports, go for a hike, visit a museum, or cook a new recipe. These activities distract from social media-induced desires and build a life that feels fulfilling offline.

Creating a Positive Online Environment: Your Financial Wellness Zone

Turning your social media environment into a positive space starts with intentionality. Follow financial educators, minimalism advocates, and personal development coaches, who often share content that can inspire you to make thoughtful spending decisions. Many of these accounts provide tips on financial planning, smart investing, and reducing waste, which can help shift your perspective from spending to saving and investing in your future.

Reflection Exercise - Social Media and Spending

- List the last five non-essential items you purchased and what inspired those purchases. How many were influenced by social media?

_____

_____

_____

- Reflect on how these purchases have contributed to your life. Do they bring you lasting happiness or satisfaction?

_____

_____

_____

- How can you change your social media feeds to support your financial goals and reduce impulsive spending?

_____

_____

_____

By engaging in such reflections, you can draw boundaries that protect your financial health from the persuasive power of social media. Remember that every dollar you don't spend on fleeting trends is a dollar you can invest in your future—whether through savings, investments, or spending on experiences that have lasting meaning in your life.

2.3 APPS AND TOOLS TO SIMPLIFY BUDGETING

If you are like us, the idea of sitting down with a stack of receipts and a calculator to manage your finances is about as appealing as watching paint dry. What if you could turn that chore into something as easy and engaging as scrolling through your social media feed? Enter the world of budgeting apps and financial tools, your new best friends in the saga of money management. These aren't just bland, number-crunching robots; they're designed to fit seamlessly into your lifestyle, offering both simplicity and a dash of fun.

Budgeting Apps: Your Financial Dashboard

Wouldn't it be nice to have a personal finance advisor who is always ready to tell you how much you can spend on those new shoes or whether you need to tighten the belt this week? That's essentially what a budgeting app does. There are several budgeting apps to choose from, so go ahead and search for those devoted YouTubers who have already done the homework for you by outlining the pros and cons of each one. Here are just a few of the options to consider: *Monarch*, *NerdWallet*, *Rocket Money*, *EveryDollar*, *YNAB* (You Need a Budget), *Quicken Simplifi*, and *PocketGuard*. Some are free to use, while others require a subscription to access more advanced features. Taking a bit of time upfront to find the best fit for you and your lifestyle is definitely worth it. It can be life-changing when you can easily make a budget and track your expenses with the touch of a button.

Custom Tools: Tailor-Made Budgeting Solutions

While apps and software are great, sometimes you need something tailor-made for your unique financial situation. That's where tools like spreadsheets come in. Google Sheets or Microsoft Excel can become powerful allies in managing your finances. You can create custom categories, formulas to calculate savings goals, and charts to visualize your progress. It's a bit more DIY, but it allows for complete customization.

Spreadsheets are especially great for those who love diving into the details. You can track fluctuations in your spending, calculate how changes in one area affect your overall budget, and experiment with different saving scenarios to see how they impact your goals. It's a more hands-on approach, but it's a perfect fit for the data nerds among us.

In short, managing your money has never been easier or more accessible. Whether you're a fan of sleek apps that do most of the work for you, comprehensive software that provides deep dives into financial planning, or custom tools that let you tweak every detail, there's something out there that fits your lifestyle. These tools simplify the process and make it more engaging, turning the daunting task of budgeting into a manageable and even enjoyable part of your daily routine. Explore what these tools have to offer, and take control of your financial future with confidence.

2.4 AVOIDING COMMON BUDGETING PITFALLS FOR TEENS AND YOUNG ADULTS

Let's face it, we'd all like budgeting to be simply lining up numbers and patting ourselves on the back for staying under budget. However, sometimes it's more like walking through a minefield where small missteps can blow our financial plans to smithereens. It's easy to slip up, especially when you're a teen or young adult balancing classes, maybe a job, and that all-important social life. Recognizing these pitfalls is the first step in dodging them. With a little foresight, you can sidestep these budget busters like a pro.

Overlooking Small Expenses: The Silent Budget Killers

Ever find yourself wondering where all your money went, even though you've been avoiding big purchases? Those small, almost invisible expenses are likely the culprits. A soft drink here, an app purchase there, a snack from the vending machine—individually, they seem inconsequential, but together, they can gnaw away at your wallet like nothing else.

The key to keeping these little spendthrifts in check is awareness. Start by tracking every penny you spend—yes, even the $2.50 on a soft drink. Use a spending tracker app or even a simple spreadsheet. This might sound monotonous, but seeing a month's worth of nickels and dimes laid out is eye-opening. Once you identify the patterns, set specific limits for these small expenses. Maybe allocate a "fun money" budget that allows for these little pleasures without letting them overrun your financial goals. It's all about balance – allowing yourself those small indulgences without letting them derail your budget.

Failing to Plan for Irregular Expenses: The Budgeting Blind Spots

Then there are those irregular expenses that don't come around every month but hit hard when they do—think about things like regular car maintenance and registration, annual subscriptions, or birthday and Christmas gifts for friends and family. These aren't surprises; they're certainties with irregular timing. Failing to plan for these can throw your budget into chaos, forcing you to dip into savings or, worse, rack up credit card debt.

To combat this, make a list of annual or semi-annual expenses you can predict. Divide the total cost by 12, and tuck away that amount each month into a dedicated savings account. This way, when the expense is due, you've got the funds ready and waiting. Knowing you'll need a new pair of sneakers for the upcoming track season and setting aside a little each month allows you to stride into the store and pick the pair you really want without sweating the price tag.

Expense	Annual Cost ($)	Monthly Savings ($)
Car Insurance	1200	100
Car Registration	240	20
Holiday Gifts	600	50
Track Sneakers	120	10
Annual Subscriptions	60	5
Savings Needed Per Month		**$185**

Neglecting Savings: The Non-negotiable Financial Pillar

Lastly, let's talk about savings. Often seen as the leftover piece of the budget pie, savings should actually be one of the first slices you cut. Neglecting to save is like skipping the foundations when building a house. Sure, you might put up the structure faster, but how long before cracks appear?

Treat savings as a **non-negotiable expense**. Decide on a percentage of your income to save each month, and stick to it as if it were a bill that must be paid. Automate your savings if you can. Set up your bank account to transfer the funds to a savings account every payday. Automation makes savings invisible and painless. It's not about how much you save initially but about developing the habit. Over time, as your income grows, you can increase the amount, building a robust financial cushion that will serve you well in emergencies and help fund larger future goals. Another savings hack for the tech-savvy is to leverage apps like *Acorns*, *Chime*, and *Greenlight* (great for kids & teens) that round up your change from everyday purchases and save the difference. You'd be surprised by how quickly those pennies can add up.

In wrapping up this chapter, let's circle back to the essence of effective budgeting for teens and young adults like you. It's not about restriction; it's about making informed choices that align with your values and goals. By being mindful of the pitfalls – those sneaky small expenses, the irregular but inevitable costs, the allure of impulse buys, and the critical role of savings, you set the stage for a financial strategy that supports not just your current needs, but also your long-term aspirations. As we transition into the next chapter, keep these insights in mind. They are the building blocks for the more advanced financial planning and decision-making we'll explore next, where we dive deeper into maximizing your financial potential through smart saving, investing and income strategies. Stay tuned, and remember that every step you take now is a step toward a financially secure and fulfilling future.

ACTION STEPS FOR BUDGETING BASICS

1. Craft Your First Budget

Set Financial Goals

- Define short-term goals (e.g., saving for a new laptop).
- Define long-term goals (e.g., saving for a car or education).

Track Income and Expenses

- List all sources of income (part-time job, freelance gigs, etc.).
- List all expenses (rent, food, subscriptions, transportation, etc.).
- Use tools like banking apps, spreadsheets, or pen and paper for accuracy.

Allocate Funds

- Prioritize essential expenses (housing, food, transportation).
- Use the 50/30/20 rule, adjusting percentages based on your needs.

2. Plan for Irregular Expenses

Identify annual or semi-annual expenses (car maintenance, subscriptions, gifts, etc.).

- Calculate the total cost and divide by 12 to determine how much to save monthly.
- Set up a dedicated savings account for these expenses.

3. Save Consistently

Treat savings as a non-negotiable expense.

- Decide on a percentage of your income to save each month.
- Automate your savings.

4. Adjust Your Budget Regularly

Review your budget monthly.

- Analyze spending patterns and adjust allocations as needed.
- Plan for unexpected expenses, and maintain a buffer.

5. Manage Small and Impulse Expenses

Track all small expenses to identify patterns.

- Set specific limits for non-essential spending.
- Use waiting periods for large purchases to avoid impulsive buys.

CHAPTER 3
MASTERING MONEY SAVING TECHNIQUES

If you want to get rich, think of saving as earning.

ANDREW CARNEGIE

Picture this: You're browsing through the latest sneaker drops online, and there's this one pair that's practically calling your name. Unfortunately, your wallet is on a strict budget of instant noodles and dreams. Before you give up and resign yourself to wearing your old, worn-out kicks, let's discuss some smart strategies to boost your savings on a low income. Learn how to make your money work harder so you can indulge in your interests without constantly feeling the pinch.

3.1 SMART SAVING STRATEGIES ON A SHOESTRING BUDGET

Saving money can sometimes feel like trying to fill a leaking bucket. You know it's smart to stash some cash for later, but the temptation to spend now can be overwhelming, especially when you're operating on a shoestring budget. Here's the scoop: saving isn't just about piling up cash for some distant, unknown future. It's about securing your peace of mind today and ensuring that you can handle whatever life throws at you tomorrow. So, how do you balance saving with living a life you enjoy now? Let's examine some strategies that can help without making you live on instant noodles (unless you're into that)

Prioritizing Savings: Why Your Future Self Will Thank You

Imagine your savings as a safety net or a launchpad; it's there to catch you if you fall and to propel you to new heights when you're ready to leap. Prioritizing savings means paying your future self first. It's tempting to think, "I'll save whatever's left at the end of the month." But let's be honest: how often is there anything left? Flipping the script means that you decide how much to save right off the bat when you plan your monthly budget, and then you adapt your spending to what remains.

To make this a habit, start small. Even a tiny amount, like 5% of your monthly income, is a solid start. The key is consistency. As your income increases, boost your savings rate proportionally. If you snag a raise or a better-paying gig, resist the urge to inflate your lifestyle in tandem. Keep your living standards steady, and funnel that extra cash into your savings. Before you know it, you'll have a tidy sum, and your future self? They're already throwing you a thank-you party.

Making Money Work for You: The Magic of Compound Interest

Now, let's talk about turning your savings into more savings without lifting a finger. Enter compound interest, which is basically your money making more money from the money it already made—yes, it's as great as it sounds. Here's the rundown: you earn interest not just on your initial savings but also on the interest that those savings earn. Over time, this snowballs, and your savings grow exponentially without additional work from you.

Here is a chart showing the magic of compounding interest over a 5-year period. Starting with a principal amount of $1,000 and an annual interest rate of 5%, you can see how the amount grows each year:

Year	Amount ($)
1	$ 1,050.00
2	$ 1,102.50
3	$ 1,157.63
4	$ 1,215.51
5	$ 1,276.28

To truly harness the power of compound interest, look for a savings account with a competitive interest rate, and let time do its thing. The key here is patience. Compound interest is a slow cooker, not a microwave, but the results are worth the wait.

Finding Extra Money to Save: Leave No Stones Unturned

Think you've tightened your belt to the last notch? Let's dig a bit deeper. There are generally overlooked money leaks in most budgets. Start by auditing your subscriptions—do you need that additional streaming plan, for instance? Next, evaluate your recurring purchases. Maybe you can swap branded products for generics, or cut down on those energy drinks. Each small saving adds up, providing more ammo for your savings arsenal. Use apps or websites to compare prices before making significant purchases to ensure that you're getting the best deal. Get inspired by frugal living gurus on

YouTube and Instagram who are willing to share all of their money-saving secrets. Find one who is in your stage of life to get the most pertinent advice. Make saving money a game. It can be thrilling to find something you use regularly for a cheaper price.

Utilizing Cashback and Rewards Programs: Get Paid to Spend

If you have to spend money, you might as well get some of it back, right? Cashback and rewards programs can be the added bonus you didn't know existed. Whether it's a credit card that gives you cash back on purchases or a loyalty program at your favorite retailer, these programs can help you recover some cash from your spending. Just be sure to pay off credit balances in full each month to avoid interest charges that could eat up your cashback rewards.

Bulk Buying and Couponing: Old School but Gold

Here's where we get a bit old-school, but trust us, Grandma was on to something. Bulk buying and couponing can significantly slash your grocery bills. Buy non-perishables in bulk when they're on sale, and hunt down digital coupons for items you regularly use. Combine coupons with store sales for genius-level savings.

Minimizing Dining Out: Home Is Where the Savings Are

Eating out is fun, but cooking at home is the secret sauce to saving dough. Home-cooked meals are generally cheaper per serving compared to restaurant meals. Start with simple recipes and batch cooking. When it comes to food, plan your meals, shop with a list, and resist those expensive snack urges. The internet is swarming with free meal plans designed for people on a budget. The practice of cooking one meal and freezing leftovers for lunches or future dinners is a lot cheaper than cooking something different every day or eating out regularly. Also, turn cooking into a social event by hosting potluck dinners with friends instead of going out. You'll save money, improve your culinary skills, and maybe impress someone special with your newfound chef prowess.

Savings Challenges: Make Saving a Sport

Inject some fun into your savings routine with challenges. Try a no-spend month on non-essentials, or set a challenge to save a certain amount in a specified period. Make it a competition with friends to see who can save the most. These challenges can turn the mundane task of saving money into a more exciting endeavor.

Celebrating Milestones

Speaking of milestones, don't forget to celebrate them! Set up mini-rewards for when you hit certain savings targets. Maybe treat yourself to a nice meal out when you've saved your first $1000 towards your car fund, or buy that pair of shoes when you successfully stick to your budget for three months straight. These celebrations act as positive reinforcement, making the act of saving feel more rewarding. Go ahead and give yourself a pat on the back to recognize the discipline it took to get there. By celebrating these wins, you reinforce the good behavior of saving and keep the motivation burning to reach the next milestone. After all, what's the fun in working toward a goal if you can't enjoy the journey along the way?

Reflection Section

Take a moment to reflect on which of these savings hacks you're excited to try first. Jot down a quick plan on how you'll implement it over the next month. Setting a clear, achievable goal can significantly increase the likelihood of sticking to your new savings strategy.

Remember, each small step is a leap towards your financial independence.

_____

_____

_____

3.2 HIGH-YIELD SAVINGS ACCOUNTS: WHAT YOU NEED TO KNOW

Alright, so imagine you've been nurturing your savings in a regular account, and it's growing, sure, but it's kind of like watching paint dry. Slow and steady. Now, picture this: what if your savings could do a bit of heavy lifting on their own, bulking up like they've been hitting the gym hard? That's where high-yield savings accounts come into play, giving your money a chance to grow faster, without you having to lift a finger.

What Are High-Yield Savings Accounts

High-yield savings accounts are like the superheroes of the banking world. Unlike their mild-mannered cousin, the traditional savings account, these accounts offer a higher interest rate. Think of it as the difference between stashing your cash under a mattress versus investing in a venture that actually pays off. While the typical savings account might offer a meager 0.01% APY (Annual Percentage Yield), a high-yield account can soar to rates around 0.50% APY or more, depending on the market. This means that for every $1,000 you save, instead of earning just 10 cents in a year, you could earn $5 or more.

Not exactly a fortune, but it's free money, and it's working on your behalf.

Benefits and Drawbacks

Now, sifting through the perks, the most glaringly obvious is that higher interest rate. It's passive income that accumulates faster than traditional savings, helping you reach financial goals more swiftly. Additionally, high-yield accounts often come with the same benefits as traditional savings accounts, like online access, transfer options, and sometimes, mobile check deposits. They make saving not just fruitful but also convenient.

However, no hero is without a flaw. High-yield accounts can come with strings attached. Some banks might require a higher minimum balance to maintain the account, or they might limit the number of free withdrawals you can make each month. And while the interest rates are attractive, they're often variable, subject to change based on the ebb and flow of the market. That means the impressive rate you sign up for might deflate a bit if the overall economic tide goes out.

Choosing the Right Account

When you're ready to pick a high-yield savings account, don't just jump at the first one with the highest interest rate. Look under the hood; check for any monthly maintenance fees or minimum balance requirements that could nibble away at your interest earnings. Also, consider the bank's reputation and customer service. You want a bank that's stable and makes you feel like a valued customer, not just an account number.

Online banks often offer higher rates than traditional brick-and-mortar banks because they have lower overhead costs. Don't shy away from them, but do your homework to ensure they're reputable.

Check user reviews, and see what other customers have to say about their reliability and service. Remember, the goal is to make your savings work harder, not to add stress to your life.

Safety and Security

One common concern about stashing your cash in any bank account, but especially in an online one, is safety. Here's the good news: most high-yield savings accounts are offered by banks insured by the Federal Deposit Insurance Corporation (FDIC), which means your money is protected up to $250,000. If you're looking at credit unions, look for accounts insured by the National Credit Union Administration (NCUA). This insurance means that even if the bank fails, your money is safe.

In summary, high-yield savings accounts can be a potent tool in your financial arsenal. They offer higher interest rates, allowing your savings to grow faster and work harder. However, they're not free from drawbacks, such as potential minimum balance requirements and fluctuating interest rates. Choosing the right account demands a balance of favorable terms and robust security. Always ensure the institution is FDIC or NCUA insured, safeguarding your hard-earned cash.

As we wrap up this exploration of high-yield savings accounts, remember they are just one piece of the complex puzzle of personal finance. They're a fantastic tool for growing your savings, but they work best when used in conjunction with other smart financial strategies like budgeting, investing, and managing debt. In the next chapter, we delve deeper into the world of credit and debt management—a crucial arena for anyone looking to build a solid financial foundation. Stay tuned to learn how to navigate these waters safely and effectively, ensuring your financial journey is not just about saving but also about thriving.

3.3 ESTABLISHING YOUR EMERGENCY FUND: HOW MUCH IS ENOUGH?

Imagine this: you wake up to find your laptop, which is practically an extension of your own limbs, has decided to play dead. No amount of coaxing or cursing brings it back to life, and just like that, you're staring down the barrel of an unexpected—and pricey—laptop replacement. That's where an emergency fund steps in, your financial superhero, ready to swoop in and save the day. This isn't just about safeguarding against tech tragedies; it's about ensuring you're covered for any of life's unpredictable expenses, from medical bills to sudden job losses.

Importance of an Emergency Fund: Your Financial Safety Net

Think of an emergency fund as your financial safety net, cushioning you from the hard falls caused by life's surprises. Without it, every unexpected expense is a potential financial disaster that could send you spiraling into debt. The peace of mind that comes from knowing you have a stash of cash reserved exclusively for emergencies is price-less. It means you're not stressing over every little hiccup because you have a backup plan. It's like knowing there's a spare tire in your trunk —it might not be exciting, but if a tire blows, you'll be patting your-self on the back instead of pulling out your hair.

Calculating Your Needs: Tailoring Your Emergency Fund

So, how much do you actually need in this fund? The one-size-fits-all answer would be handy, but your emergency fund should reflect your personal circumstances. A good rule of thumb is to aim for three to six months' worth of living expenses. This range gives you a buffer substantial enough to handle most of what life could throw your way without leaving your finances in shambles.

Start by detailing your monthly necessities—rent, food, utilities, and any other must-haves. Don't include luxuries; sushi nights and streaming subscriptions don't count. Once you've got a total, multiply that by how many months you want your safety net to cover. If your monthly burn is $1,000 and you're aiming for a three-month fund, you'll need $3,000 stashed away. This number isn't static, though. Life changes, and so should your emergency fund. Regularly revisiting your calculations ensures your fund keeps pace with your life.

Starting Small: Building Your Fund Bit by Bit

The idea of saving thousands might sound like climbing Everest in flip-flops, especially if you're not swimming in cash. But here's the kicker—you don't have to fund this overnight. Starting small is perfectly fine. The key is consistency. Even a small amount, say $50 from each paycheck, begins to build momentum over time. Consider setting up an automatic transfer to a dedicated emergency savings account each payday. It's out of your hands before you can even think about spending it, padding your emergency fund without pinching your lifestyle.

Keeping It Accessible: Smart Storage for Your Emergency Fund

Now, let's talk about where to park this fund. Accessibility is crucial —you don't want your funds locked up when you need them most. However, too easy access can be a temptation trap, leading you to dip into it for non-emergencies. A high-yield savings account strikes a good balance. It keeps your money separate from your day-to-day funds but accessible enough that you can get to it quickly when needed. Plus, it earns a bit of interest, helping your emergency fund grow passively.

Moreover, resist the urge to invest your emergency fund in the stock market. High returns might sound enticing, but the market's volatility could shrink your fund just when you need it most. Stick to options where your money is protected and the value doesn't fluctuate, ensuring that every penny you save is ready to protect you when the storm hits.

Jake, a 25-year-old recent college graduate, established an emergency fund after getting his first job. He calculated his monthly expenses and set a goal to save $4,500 for a three-month buffer. By setting aside $100 from each paycheck into a high-yield savings account, Jake gradually built up his fund. When his car suddenly broke down, requiring costly repairs, Jake was able to use his emergency fund to cover the expenses without stress. This financial safety net allowed him to handle the unexpected cost smoothly, providing him with peace of mind even when life was unpredictable.

By steadily building and smartly positioning your emergency fund, you create a financial bulwark that shields you from life's unforeseen expenses. Whether it's a medical emergency, urgent home repairs, or an abrupt job loss, your emergency fund is your first line of financial defense, ensuring that these shocks don't derail your financial stability or long-term goals. Instead of scrambling in panic, you'll handle life's surprises with a calm confidence, secure in the knowledge that your finances are under control, no matter what happens.

In the next chapter, we dive deeper into the world of credit and debt management—a crucial arena for anyone looking to build a solid financial foundation. Before we depart the topic of saving, though, look through this checklist for a quick refresher on the key ideas.

ACTION STEPS FOR MASTERING MONEY SAVING TECHNIQUES

1. Prioritize Savings

- Set a savings goal (e.g., 5% of income).
- Adjust your savings rate as your income increases.

2. Utilize Compound Interest

- Open a high-yield savings account.
- Regularly deposit money to benefit from compound interest.

3. Find Extra Money to Save

- Audit expenses for unnecessary costs.
- Follow frugal living tips and find deals.

4. Establish Your Emergency Fund

- Aim for 3-6 months' living expenses.
- Use a high-yield savings account.

CHAPTER 4
CREDIT AND DEBT MANAGEMENT

Debt erases freedom more surely than anything else.

MARRYN SOMERSET WEBB

Understanding the difference between good debt and bad debt is essential for sound financial management. Good debt refers to borrowing that can enhance your financial future, such as student loans, mortgages, or business loans. In these cases, the borrowed funds are used to invest in assets that have the potential to grow in value or generate income. Conversely, bad debt usually means borrowing money for things that lose value quickly or aren't really necessary. This includes using credit cards for everyday shopping or taking out expensive loans for things you don't really need. This kind of debt doesn't help your financial situation, and it can often trap you in a cycle of paying off more and more debt. Recognizing and differentiating between these types of debt can help you make smarter financial decisions and build a more secure economic future.

4.1 BUILDING CREDIT FROM SCRATCH: MORE THAN JUST A NUMBER

A credit score, in its essence, is a measure of your creditworthiness. Once you move out of your parent's house, your credit score will be a silent companion for the rest of your life. It can help you or hurt you, and it all depends on the financial choices you make. Banks and lenders use this number to decide if lending you money is a risky bet or a safe one. This score is calculated based on your financial behaviors—like those times you paid (or didn't pay) your bills on time, the mountain (or molehill) of debt you owe, and the length of your credit history. This is where being a financial "newbie" can be a bit of a disadvantage. Lenders love a long, positive track record because it gives them a sense of your good money management habits over time.

Your credit score is a number that ranges typically from 300 to 850. The higher your score, the more financially trustworthy you are perceived to be.

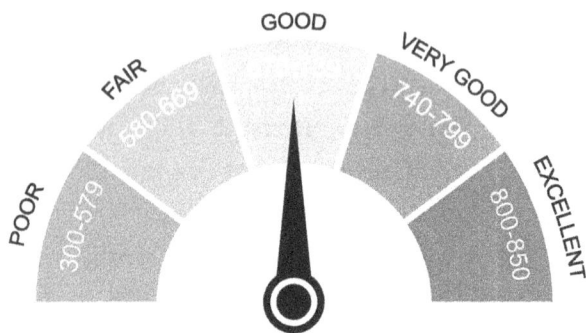

CREDIT SCORE

Why does this number matter? Your credit score influences your ability to borrow money, secure a place to live, and sometimes even land a job. It can also affect your insurance rates, security deposits on rentals, and even your eligibility for cell phone contracts.

A good credit score can mean lower interest rates when you borrow money, translating to thousands of dollars saved over time. On the flip side, a low score can lead to higher interest rates, hefty security deposits, or outright rejections. Britton and Adam both borrowed $10,000 to buy their first car. With good credit, Britton pays $181.92 per month for his car loan, totaling $10,915.20 over five years. Adam, with bad credit, pays $222.44 per month, totaling $13,346.40 over the same period. Due to his lower credit score, Adam pays $40.52 more per month and $2,431.20 more than Britton over the life of the loan. When we say that having good credit will save you a lot of money, we really mean it!

Starting Points for Building Credit: Planting the Seeds

Building credit might seem like a catch-22—you need credit to build credit. So, where do you begin? One of the safest starting points is with a secured credit card. This is a type of credit card that's backed by a cash deposit from you, which typically sets your credit limit. Think of it as training wheels for credit usage; it helps you build your score without the risk of falling into debt, provided you manage it responsibly.

Student credit cards are another great option, especially designed for young adults like you. They typically have lower credit limits and more lenient approval criteria, tailored to those with little to no credit history. Some even offer rewards like cash back on groceries or gas, making them not only a tool for building credit but also for saving on everyday expenses.

Responsible Credit Habits: The Building Blocks

Once you've got your credit card, it's about spending wisely. The golden rule? Always pay your bills on time! Late payments can knock points off your credit score faster than you can say "due date." Set up reminders or automate your payments to dodge this bullet. Also, pay off your credit card every single month. Credit card interest rates are no joke (We're talking between 18% and 29% or even higher.), so only spend as much as you can easily pay at the end of the month.

When it comes to your credit rating, there's the amount you owe, which sounds straightforward but has a twist. It's not just how much you owe; it's how much you owe compared to your available credit, a ratio known as your "credit utilization." Maxing out your credit cards is a red flag to lenders, signaling potential desperation. A good rule of thumb is to keep your utilization under 30%. For example, if your credit limit is $1,000, try to keep the balance you owe below $300.

Monitoring and Understanding Your Credit Report: Your Financial Mirror

Once a year, you can get a free credit report from the three major credit reporting bureaus—Equifax, Experian, and TransUnion. It's like an annual check-up for your financial health. Here's a quick checklist to guide you through reviewing your credit report:

1. **Confirm Your Personal Info**: Ensure your name, address, and employment information are correct.
2. **Review Credit Accounts**: Verify that all accounts listed are yours and that the details, like balances and payment histories, are accurate.

3. **Spot Errors and Fraud**: Look for any accounts you don't recognize or errors in reporting. These could be signs of fraud or mistakes dragging down your score.
4. **Plan Corrections**: If you find errors, report them immediately to the credit bureau and the institution that provided the incorrect information.

Understanding and regularly checking your credit report empowers you to take control of your credit score. It allows you to spot issues early and to track how your financial behaviors affect your credit over time. Just as you wouldn't ignore a check engine light in your car, don't ignore your credit report. It's an important tool in maintaining and improving your financial health.

By grasping the importance of your credit score, you're laying down a solid financial foundation. Things like using the right financial tools, adopting responsible credit habits, and regularly monitoring your credit report are your stepping stones through the world of credit to survive and thrive. They will enable you to leverage your financial reputation to achieve your personal and financial goals.

Let's look at the stories of Jason and Mark, two best friends who grew up as neighbors. As they ventured into adulthood, their paths toward financial understanding diverged significantly.

Jason, always meticulous and forward-thinking, understood the importance of a strong credit history early on. He applied for his first credit card during college, using it strictly for necessary purchases and paying the balance in full each month. By the time he graduated, he had already established a respectable credit score.

On the other hand, Mark, easygoing and spontaneous, rarely considered the long-term implications of his financial decisions. He had little understanding of how credit worked and did not see the urgency in learning about it. Utilities and other bills were often paid late when he remembered them at the last minute. The concept of a credit score was foreign to him, so he never bothered to check his score until it became necessary.

The day came when both friends, now in their late twenties, decided to buy homes in their hometown. Jason approached the bank with confidence, armed with a strong credit score and a substantial down payment saved from years of careful financial planning. The bank offered him a favorable mortgage rate, making his dream of owning a home a smooth reality.

Mark's experience, however, was starkly different. Upon applying for a mortgage, he was shocked to find his credit score was poor. The bank explained how his habitual late payments and lack of credit history had negatively impacted his score. As a result, he faced high interest rates that he hadn't anticipated, and the loan terms offered were far from favorable. Struggling to secure a mortgage, Mark realized that he had to delay his plans for homeownership and instead work on repairing his credit, which meant months, if not years, of diligent attention to his finances.

Their contrasting experiences reinforced the value of financial literacy and planning. While Jason enjoyed the comfort of his new home, Mark embarked on a journey to rebuild his financial health, hopeful that one day, he, too, would be ready to step into a home of his own.

4.2 FINANCIAL STRATEGIES FOR COLLEGE: MINIMIZING DEBT

While education costs can be considered "good debt" because you are investing in your future earning potential, getting a degree with little or no debt at all is even better. College students have many avenues for finding scholarships and grants to offset tuition costs. Here are some of the best ways:

1. **College Financial Aid Offices**: Start by contacting your college's financial aid office. They can provide information on institutional scholarships and grants offered by the college itself and guidance on how to apply for external scholarships.

2. **Scholarship Search Engines**: Utilize online scholarship search engines such as *Fastweb, Scholarships.com*, and *College Board's Scholarship Search*. These platforms allow you to create a profile and match you with scholarships that fit your background, interests, and qualifications.

3. **Community Organizations and Foundations**: Many community organizations, foundations, and local businesses offer scholarships to students in their area. Check with community centers, religious organizations, Rotary Clubs, and other local groups to inquire about scholarship opportunities.

4. **Professional Associations**: If you're pursuing a specific field of study or career path, look for opportunities offered by professional associations related to that field. These organizations often provide scholarships to support students pursuing careers in their industry.

5. **Employer and Parental Benefits**: Some employers offer tuition assistance programs for employees or their dependents. Check with your employer or parent's employer to explore these options. Additionally, family members of veterans or active-duty military service personnel may be eligible for educational benefits through programs such as the GI Bill.

6. **Government Grants and Programs**: Explore government-funded grants and programs, such as the Pell Grant for undergraduate students with financial need or state-specific grants and scholarships. Visit the Federal Student Aid website (fafsa.gov) for information on federal grants and how to apply.

7. **Online Platforms and Crowdfunding**: Consider using online crowdfunding platforms like GoFundMe or crowdfunding features on scholarship websites to raise funds for your education. Share your story and goals to attract donors who may be willing to support your educational expenses.

8. **Essay Contests and Competitions**: Keep an eye out for essay contests, competitions, and other opportunities that offer scholarships as prizes. Many organizations and companies sponsor contests on various topics, providing scholarships to winners.

9. **High School Guidance Counselors**: If you're still in high school, reach out to your guidance counselor for assistance in finding and applying for scholarships. They may have resources and information on local and national scholarships available to graduating seniors.

10. **Online Research and Networking**: Conduct thorough online research and network with peers, mentors, and educators to uncover lesser-known scholarship opportunities. Stay proactive and persistent in your search efforts to maximize your chances of securing financial aid.

Remember that even if you have already started college, you can continue to apply for scholarships until you graduate. The time you spend searching for and applying for scholarships will pay for itself. Even if you aren't the smartest kid in the class or a successful college athlete, there are plenty of scholarships for everyone.

4.3 STUDENT LOANS: BORROWING WISELY AND REPAYMENT STRATEGIES

Perhaps you've got some scholarships and/or grant money, and you're working hard at a part-time job, but it still won't be enough to cover everything. Now what? When borrowing money for college, aim for a loan amount that you can comfortably repay based on your future earning potential. A common guideline is to ensure that your total student loan debt does not exceed your expected annual starting salary after graduation. This can help prevent overwhelming debt burdens and make your loan payments manageable.

As for the "magic ratio" of future earning potential to the loan amount, there isn't a specific universal formula since it can vary widely depending on individual circumstances, such as career choice, earning potential in specific fields, and personal financial goals. However, a commonly suggested guideline is to aim for a debt-to-income ratio (the ratio of your total monthly debt payments to your gross monthly income) of 36% or lower. Remember that this includes all your debt, not just student loans.

To determine how much you can make in different fields, you can research average salaries and earning potential for various careers. There are several resources you can use:

1. **Bureau of Labor Statistics (BLS)**: The BLS provides comprehensive data on employment, wages, and projections for various occupations in the United States. You can find detailed information on median salaries, job outlook, and educational requirements for different professions.
2. **Salary Websites**: Websites like *Glassdoor*, *PayScale*, and *Indeed* offer salary data based on user-reported salaries and employer-reported salary ranges. These platforms can

provide insights into the average salaries for specific job titles and industries.

3. **Career Services**: Many colleges and universities have departments providing resources and guidance on career exploration, job search strategies, and salary negotiation. They may offer access to salary surveys or alumni data to help you understand earning potential in different fields.

4. **Professional Associations**: Industry-specific professional associations often conduct salary surveys and publish reports on compensation trends within their respective fields. Joining these associations or accessing their resources online can provide valuable insights into salary expectations for different occupations.

By researching salary data and considering your career goals and financial circumstances, you can make informed decisions about how much to borrow for college and which career paths may offer the best return on your investment.

It's tempting to view student loans as free money but remember that this is a loan—not a gift. You'll need to pay back every dime, with a hearty side of interest, even if you drop out before getting your degree. Start by breaking down your college expenses: tuition, books, housing, food, and, yes, even some cash for fun. Then, subtract any scholarships, grants, and part-time job earnings. The goal here isn't to fund a lavish college lifestyle but to cover your necessities. A practical approach is to budget strictly and to borrow conservatively. Consider used or electronic textbooks, opt for a less expensive meal plan, or choose budget-friendly housing. Every dollar you don't borrow is one you won't have to pay back with interest later.

When choosing between federal and private loans, think of it as choosing between a fixed-rate mortgage and an adjustable-rate mortgage.

- **Federal loans** are like the fixed-rate option. They're generally safer, with fixed interest rates and more flexible repayment options. They also come with benefits like deferment, forbearance, and access to various repayment plans, including income-driven repayment plans that adjust your monthly payments based on your income.
- **Private loans**, on the other hand, can be more like an adjustable-rate mortgage. They might offer lower interest rates initially, but those rates can fluctuate. Also, they often require a credit check. Additionally, private loans don't usually offer the same breadth of repayment options and protections as federal loans. They're more rigid, and if you find yourself struggling financially, you might not have as much wiggle room.

When it comes to repayment, let's talk strategy. Once you're out of college, you'll likely look at many repayment plans. Here's where it gets really personal. You'll need to pick a plan that suits your financial situation and your stress tolerance. Standard repayment plans will generally have you debt-free faster, but the payments can be hefty. Graduated repayment plans start with lower payments that increase over time, hopefully alongside your salary. Then there's the income-driven repayment, which adjusts your monthly payments based on your income and family size, often extending the life of your loan but reducing monthly payments.

For those entering public service, loan forgiveness might sound like a financial fairy godmother. Programs like Public Service Loan Forgiveness (PSLF) can erase remaining debt after 10 years of qualifying payments for those working in government, non-profit, or other qualifying public service jobs. However, this program has a maze of eligibility requirements—from the type of loans you have to the specifics of your employment contract—making it crucial to ensure you're ticking all the right boxes from the get-go.

Navigating student loans is no walk in the park, but with a clear understanding of your needs, careful borrowing, choosing the right type of loan, and strategizing your repayment, you can manage your education debt without letting it manage you. Remember that the decisions you make about student loans can impact your financial landscape far into the future. Therefore, consider your options carefully, plan with precision, and, when in doubt, reach out to a financial advisor. You are setting up a financial foundation that will support you well beyond your college years.

Financial Success Stories and Cautionary Tales: Lessons in College Financial Management

Students with Too Much Student Debt:

1. Drake: Drake graduated with a degree in art history and accumulated $100,000 in student loan debt. Due to a competitive job market and lower earning potential in the field, Drake struggled to find a job that paid more than $30,000 per year. With a debt burden far exceeding his annual income, Drake faced significant challenges in managing loan payments while covering basic living expenses.
2. Sarah: Sarah pursued a graduate degree in a specialized field, taking out $150,000 in student loans to finance her education. Despite completing her program and securing a job in her field, Sarah's starting salary was lower than anticipated due to unexpected industry dynamics and the fact that she was offered only entry-level positions. With a debt-to-income ratio well above the recommended levels,

Sarah found herself financially strained and unable to make meaningful progress in paying down her student debt.

Students with Manageable Student Debt:

1. Marcus: Marcus attended a public university and carefully managed his finances throughout college. He received scholarships and grants, worked part-time during the school year, and interned during the summers to gain experience in his field. By graduation, Marcus had accumulated only $20,000 in student loans. After securing a job in his field with a starting salary of $50,000 per year, Marcus was able to comfortably manage his loan payments while still saving for the future.
2. Sophia: Sophia chose to attend a community college for the first two years of her undergraduate education to save on tuition costs. She then transferred to a four-year university to complete her degree, minimizing her student loan debt. By graduation, Sophia owed $30,000 in student loans. With a degree in a high-demand field and a starting salary of $60,000 per year, Sophia's debt-to-income ratio remained manageable, allowing her to make steady progress in repaying her loans while maintaining a comfortable standard of living.

These examples illustrate the importance of considering earning potential, loan amounts, and financial management strategies when making decisions about student loan borrowing. By choosing fields with solid job prospects and being strategic and proactive in managing finances during college, students can minimize their debt burdens and achieve financial stability after graduation.

4.4 THE TRUTH ABOUT CREDIT CARDS: BENEFITS AND TRAPS

Navigating credit card offers can feel a bit like decoding an ancient script—full of terms and conditions that seem designed to confuse rather than clarify. Let's decode some of these cryptic messages, starting with the ever-present APR, or Annual Percentage Rate. Picture APR as the price tag of borrowing money on your credit card. It's the rate at which interest will pile up on any balances, or the amount you still owe that carries over from month to month. Lower APRs are like finding a designer jacket on clearance—it means less debt accumulating each month you don't pay off your full balance.

Then, there are annual fees and rewards programs. Annual fees are straightforward—it's what you pay each year to use the card. Whether this fee is worth it often hinges on the rewards program linked to the card. Rewards programs can offer travel miles, cash back, or points redeemable at various retailers. Here's the kicker: if you're paying a hefty annual fee to earn rewards, you need to be sure you're actually getting more in rewards value than you're shelling out. It's like buying a gym membership—if you're not going often enough to justify the cost, it's money down the drain.

Now, let's talk about the double-edged sword of compound interest. When it works in your favor, such as in a high-yield savings account, it's like having a golden goose that lays golden eggs. But in the world of credit card debt, it's more like an unpleasant snowball rolling downhill, growing bigger and faster as it goes. Here's how it plays out. You don't pay off the entire amount, so you carry a balance owed, and interest is charged. Next month, you get charged interest not only on the original amount owed but also on the interest that was added the previous month. This continues month after month. Before you know it, what started as a manageable amount can balloon into a daunting debt.

Navigating this terrain requires a map and some savvy travel tips. For starters, always strive to pay off the card in full each month. If this is too much, try to pay more than the minimum. Minimum payments are like putting a Band-Aid on a leaky pipe—they're a temporary fix that doesn't solve the problem and often ends up costing more in the long run. By paying only the minimum, you mainly pay off the interest, not the principal. That means it takes longer and costs more to clear your debt. Let's look at Kendra, who had $1,000 of credit card debt with 18% interest. She made the minimum monthly payments for two years but was shocked to discover that she still owed $886.55 after 24 payments totaling $453.39. Have you ever run on a treadmill? This is what Kendra was doing. She was putting in the effort but not actually moving forward. Clearing debt from credit cards will save you hundreds, if not thousands, of dollars and should be a top priority.

Late fees are another pitfall. Miss a payment deadline, and you're not just facing a fee. Your interest rate could skyrocket, and your credit score might take a hit. Setting up reminders or automating your payments can keep you on track and out of the late fee trap.

Maximizing the benefits of credit cards without falling into debt is akin to playing a strategic game where planning moves ahead is crucial. Use your card for regular purchases you'd make anyway and have the cash to cover, like groceries or gas. This way, you earn rewards without spending extra. Then, pay off the balance in full each month. This strategy requires discipline but pays off by building your credit score, avoiding interest, and accumulating rewards—all without accruing debt.

Credit cards are tests of your financial discipline. Used wisely, they can be powerful allies in building your credit and reaping rewards. But without careful management, they can become quicksand for your finances, pulling you into a debt spiral that's tough to escape.

Like any powerful tool, the key lies in knowing how to wield it to your advantage—maximizing benefits while sidestepping the traps set along the way.

4.5 MANAGING DEBT WITHOUT DERAILING YOUR DREAMS

We hope that after reading this book, you will never find yourself in crippling debt, but sometimes life happens, and it's good to have a few skills up your sleeves to get you out of money trouble. Your financial dreams might feel more like distant fairy tales when you're deep in debt. Here's the secret: with the right strategies and a bit of grit, you can navigate out of debt and back on the path to achieving your dreams. Let's explore two popular methods to tackle debt: the **Debt Snowball** and **Debt Avalanche** methods.

- The **Debt Snowball** method is like training for a marathon by first running a lap around your block. You start with your smallest debt, regardless of interest rate, and pay as much as you can toward it while maintaining minimum payments on other debts. Once that first debt is out of the picture, you take the amount you were paying on it and add it to the minimum payment on your next smallest debt. This process creates a "snowball effect" as each debt gets eliminated, and your available capital for the next one increases. It's psychologically gratifying—seeing debts disappear quickly boosts your morale, keeping you motivated.
- Contrast this with the **Debt Avalanche** method, which might be likened to tackling the steepest part of the climb first. Here, you prioritize debts with the highest interest rates, regardless of the balance. You make minimum payments on all other debts and use any remaining funds to

clear the costliest debt first. This method can save you money in the long term because you're reducing the amount of high-interest debt faster. However, it requires patience since it might take longer to see your first debt fully paid off, which can be a motivational challenge.

Negotiating with creditors can also be a game-changer in your debt repayment strategy. Think of it as seeking a truce with your opponents. It's possible to negotiate lower interest rates or settlement amounts. Start by reviewing your financial situation thoroughly; knowing exactly what you can afford to pay is crucial. Approach your creditors with honesty and clarity about your situation. Many are willing to consider lower interest rates, extended payment terms, or even reducing the principal amount if it increases the likelihood of repayment. Being proactive and transparent can lead to more manageable repayment terms.

Maintaining an emergency fund plays a critical role in debt management. It's your financial safety net, designed to catch you in case of unexpected expenses without further sinking into debt. Without it, any sudden expense—be it a car repair or a medical bill—can force you back into the debt cycle. Aim to build and keep an emergency fund that covers at least three to six months of living expenses. This fund ensures that you can stick to your debt repayment plan without interruption, providing peace of mind as you work toward becoming debt-free.

Lifestyle changes are often necessary to accelerate debt repayment. This might mean re-evaluating your spending habits—dining out less frequently, cutting down on shopping sprees, or opting for more cost-effective entertainment options. Each dollar saved can be redirected toward paying off your debt. Also, consider ways to increase your income—taking on freelance work, a part-time job, or selling items you no longer need. The additional cash flow can significantly speed up your debt repayment timeline.

Staying motivated throughout this journey is critical. Debt repayment can be a long and challenging road, and it's easy to feel disheartened. Keep your goals in sight—remind yourself why you're working hard to get out of debt, whether it's buying a home, investing in your education, or simply enjoying a stress-free life. Celebrate small victories along the way. Each debt cleared is a step closer to your financial independence. Stay connected with supportive friends or online communities who are also working toward similar financial goals. Their encouragement and advice can be invaluable as you navigate your way out of debt.

As this chapter on managing debt concludes, remember that the path out of debt is traveled one step at a time. By choosing the right strategy, whether it's the snowball or avalanche method, negotiating wisely with creditors, maintaining an emergency fund, making smart lifestyle choices, and keeping your spirits high, you are setting yourself up for success. These efforts will not only help you manage and overcome your debt, but also empower you to rebuild and reclaim your financial freedom.

ACTION STEPS FOR CREDIT AND DEBT MANAGEMENT

1. Build and Maintain a Good Credit Score

- Apply for a secured credit card or a student credit card to start building credit.
- Always pay your bills on time to avoid late payments.
- Keep your credit utilization below 30%.

2. Monitor Your Credit Report Regularly

- Obtain a free credit report annually from each of the three major credit bureaus.
- Verify that all personal information and account details are accurate.
- Report any errors or signs of fraud immediately.

3. Strategize for Minimizing College Debt

- Apply for scholarships and grants through college financial aid offices, community organizations, and sources found through online search engines.
- Utilize tuition assistance programs from employers or parental benefits.
- Borrow conservatively and focus on necessary expenses.

4. Manage Student Loans Wisely

- Aim for a loan amount that does not exceed your expected annual starting salary.
- Choose federal loans for their fixed interest rates and flexible repayment options.
- Explore repayment plans and loan forgiveness programs that best fit your financial situation.

5. Use Credit Cards Responsibly

- Pay off your credit card balance in full each month to avoid interest charges.
- Avoid carrying a high balance relative to your credit limit.
- Set up payment reminders or automate payments to prevent late fees.

6. Develop Debt Repayment Strategies

- Consider the Debt Snowball method to quickly eliminate small debts for a motivational boost.
- Use the Debt Avalanche method to save money by paying off high-interest debts first.
- Negotiate with creditors for lower interest rates or more manageable repayment terms.

7. Maintain an Emergency Fund

- Save three to six months' worth of living expenses to handle unexpected costs without accruing more debt.
- Keep the fund in a high-yield savings account for easy access and growth.

MAKE A DIFFERENCE WITH YOUR REVIEW
UNLOCK THE POWER OF GENEROSITY

"Helping one person might not change the whole world, but it could change the world for one person."

People who give without expectation live longer, happier lives and often find more success. So if we've got a shot at that during our time together, let's make it happen.

Our mission is to make financial literacy accessible to everyone. Everything we do stems from that mission. And the only way for us to accomplish that mission is by reaching...well...everyone.

This is where you come in. Most people do, in fact, judge a book by its cover (and its reviews). So here's my ask on behalf of a struggling teen or young adult you've never met:

Please help that young reader by leaving this book a review.

Your gift costs no money and takes less than 60 seconds but can change someone's life forever.

Scan the QR code to leave your review on Amazon

If you feel good about helping a faceless young adult, you are my kind of person. Welcome to the club. You're one of us.

Thank you from the bottom of my heart. Now, back to our regularly scheduled programming.

https://amzn.to/472gr69

CHAPTER 5
INVESTING FOR BEGINNERS

Investing is not nearly as difficult as it looks. Successful investing involves doing a few things right and avoiding serious mistakes.

JACK BOGLE

So, you've saved up some cash, and now you're staring at your bank balance, thinking, "What's next?" It's like being all dressed up with nowhere to go. Welcome to the world of investing, where your money doesn't just sit there looking pretty—it gets to work, potentially multiplying like rabbits in the spring. Let's demystify this whole investing concept, starting from the basics and ensuring you won't feel like you're trying to read a map upside down.

5.1 YOUR FIRST INVESTMENT: STARTING SMALL

The Power of Micro-Investing: Big Dreams From Small Starts

Imagine if saving for your investment portfolio was as easy as rounding up your smoothie purchase and tossing the spare change into a growing money mountain. That's micro-investing—no need for big lump sums, just steady trickles that build up over time. It's perfect if you're not ready to dive into the deep end with large amounts of cash. Think of it like planting seeds in various pots— some might grow more than others, but all you need to start is a little soil and a few seeds, so you're not out very much over those that don't do well.

Micro-investing platforms have sprouted up all over, making it ridiculously easy to start. They work by rounding up your purchases to the nearest dollar and investing the difference. So, when you buy a burger for $5.75, that extra 25 cents gets invested. Over time, and with enough burgers, those quarters build a respectable portfolio. It's investing at a snail's pace, but remember that even snails reach the finish line.

Choosing the Right Platforms: Where to Plant Your Money Seeds

Not all micro-investing platforms are created equal, and choosing where to park your hard-earned cash can feel as daunting as picking a film on movie night. What should you look for?

Start with fees. Some apps charge monthly fees, while others take a percentage of your portfolio. It's like a cover charge at a club, so make sure it's worth what you're getting.

Next, consider features. Some apps offer automatic rebalancing, while others let you pick specific stocks or funds. Think about how much control you want and how much you're willing to learn.

User experience is also key. An app that's a nightmare to navigate can be a dealbreaker. Look for intuitive design and clear instructions. It's supposed to make investing easier, not give you a headache.

Lastly, check out reviews and ratings. They can provide insights into reliability and customer satisfaction. It's like checking a new movie's rating before you decide to watch it in the theater.

Automating Investments: Set It, Forget It, Let It Grow

If micro-investing is the first step, automating your investments is the power walk. By setting up automatic transfers to your investment account, you ensure consistent growth without thinking about it. It's like a gym membership for your wealth—regular workouts without requiring you to set reminders to hit the gym. Most platforms allow you to set up weekly, biweekly, or monthly transfers so you can tailor the flow to match your income cycle.

This approach taps into the magic of dollar-cost averaging. This means you invest a fixed amount regularly, regardless of the market's ups and downs. Sometimes, you'll buy when prices are high, and other times when they're low. Over time, these averages work out to potentially lower the cost of investing. It's like buying your favorite snacks, whether on sale or not, because you know you'll eat them eventually.

Risk and Return: Balancing Act on a Tightrope

Investing isn't just about watching your money grow; it's about managing how much uncertainty you can stomach. Micro-investing generally involves smaller amounts, so while the dollar risk is low, the percentage risk can be high, especially if you're dipping toes into volatile markets. Understanding this balance is crucial. Most apps provide some guidance, but doing a bit of homework on risk tolerance can save you some nail-biting moments.

Think about how you'd feel if you woke up to find your investment halved. If that thought gives you a cold sweat, you might want to stick to safer, albeit potentially lower-return options. Conversely, if you're the financial equivalent of a thrill-seeker, you might be okay with riskier investments that offer higher returns. Knowing where you stand on this spectrum is key to making investment choices that won't keep you up at night.

Setting Investment Goals: Your Financial Roadmap

Investment goals are your financial destination. Without them, you're just wandering through the wilderness of options without a clear path. Start by defining what you're investing for. Is it a big trip? A new car? Retirement? Each goal might require a different investment strategy and timeline. Short-term goals usually need safer investments that are easy to access quickly, while you can afford to be more aggressive with long-term goals if you have time to ride out market fluctuations.

Once your goals are set, consider how much risk you're willing to take and how much you need to invest regularly to meet your goals. This might require some adjustments along the way as your goals or financial situation changes, but having a clear blueprint from the start can make the journey less daunting and a lot more rewarding. Remember that every investor started somewhere, and with these steps, you're already on your way to growing your wealth. Take a deep breath, and let's dive into the world of investments, where your money doesn't just sit idle—it grows, changes, and ultimately works for you, paving the way toward financial independence and security.

5.2 NAVIGATING THE STOCK MARKET: FIRST-TIME INVESTOR'S GUIDE

So, you've decided to try the stock market, where fortunes can be made and, yes, sometimes lost. Before you dive in, let's get a lay of the land, or rather, a lay of the market. Essentially, the stock market is where the magic of buying and selling shares of companies happens. Think of it as a giant, complex network where everyone from big-time investors to everyday folks come to trade pieces of businesses. These shares represent a slice of ownership in a company. When you buy a share, you're betting on the company's future success. If the company does well, the value of your shares might increase, and if it doesn't, the opposite happens.

Understanding this marketplace's role in the economy is important. It's more than individual gains; the stock market is a barometer of economic health. When the market is up, it often reflects confidence in the economy. Companies use the capital (money collected from selling shares) to innovate, expand, and hire more people, fueling economic growth. Conversely, a downturn might indicate economic troubles on the horizon. Investing in the stock market is a bit like planting a garden in your community; you're contributing to and benefiting from the economic ecosystem.

Now, let's talk about how you actually read this market. You're not alone if you've ever glanced at a stock chart and felt like you were trying to read hieroglyphics. Stock charts can look intimidating, with their lines, bars, and colors, but they're really just a way to track the performance of a stock over time. The most common type is the line chart or line graph, showing the closing price of a stock over a set period. What you're looking for are trends—does the stock generally go up, or does it steadily fall? Is it volatile, with big peaks and troughs, or stable? Learning to read these charts can help you make more informed decisions about when to buy or sell.

Several reliable platforms and websites offer comprehensive charting tools. Some popular options are *Yahoo Finance*, *Google Finance*, *TradingView*, *Bloomberg*, *MarketWatch*, and *MSN Money*.

Understanding diversification is your next step. There's an old saying, "Don't put all your eggs in one basket," and it couldn't be truer in the world of investing. Diversification is about spreading your investments across various assets—different stocks, industries, and even types of investments, like bonds or real estate. This strategy helps mitigate risk. If one investment tanks, others in different sectors or asset classes might hold steady or even increase. Think of it as a financial safety net, allowing you to manage potential losses more smoothly without it being a total wipeout.

For beginners, knowing whether to go long or short is like deciding whether you're in for a marathon or a sprint. Long-term investment strategies involve buying stocks with the intention of holding onto them for years or even decades. You're looking for companies you believe will grow steadily over time, benefiting from the wonders of compound growth. On the other hand, short-term strategies might involve buying and selling stocks over a shorter period, capitalizing on market fluctuations. Both approaches have their merits and risks, and your choice should align with your financial goals, timeline, and, importantly, your comfort with risk.

Navigating the stock market is an exhilarating part of building your investment portfolio. It requires patience, a cool head, and a willingness to learn continuously. Whether you're looking at trends on a stock chart, picking a diverse set of investments, or deciding on your investment timeline, each step you take is building your competence and confidence in handling market dynamics. Remember that every investor started somewhere, and each had their first encounter with a stock chart, their first trade, and their first lesson in diversification. By starting small, staying informed, and sticking to your strategy, you're well on your way to becoming a savvy market participant.

5.3 BONDS, MUTUAL FUNDS, AND ETFS: WHAT'S RIGHT FOR YOU?

Understanding Bonds: Your Portfolio's Safety Net

Think of bonds as the chill, reliable friends in your investment circle —the ones you invite over when you need a break from the high-energy, unpredictable ones (I'm looking at you, stocks.). Bonds are essentially loans you give to governments or corporations, and in return, they promise to pay you back on a fixed schedule with interest. It's like lending money to a friend who insists on paying you back with a little extra for your trust.

There are a few different types of bonds to choose from, each with its own level of "chill." Government bonds are considered super safe; they're backed by the government, which makes them the equivalent of your friend who always shows up on time. Then there are corporate bonds, which are a bit riskier but offer higher interest rates, kind of like that friend who's a blast to hang out with but sometimes cancels at the last minute. Municipal bonds are another option, generally safe with the perk of being tax-exempt, making them the financially savvy friend of the group.

Integrating bonds into your portfolio can be a smart move, especially if you're the type who likes a bit of predictability in your financial life. They provide a steady income through interest payments, and because they're generally less volatile than stocks, they can help smooth out the bumps when the stock market gets a bit too wild. It's about balance—having enough excitement to keep things interesting but enough stability not to lose sleep over your investments.

Mutual Funds Explained: Pooling for Power

Now, let's talk mutual funds, which are like going in on a giant potluck dinner. Everyone brings a dish (or in this case, money), and you all get to share in a diverse feast of investments that none of you could have whipped up on your own. Managed by professionals who decide which stocks, bonds, or other assets to invest in, mutual funds allow you to own a small piece of a big portfolio.

The beauty of mutual funds lies in their diversity. They naturally spread out your risk because they invest in a broad range of assets. It's like diversifying your dinner spread; if the lasagna turns out a bit bland, there's still chicken, salad, and dessert to enjoy. For you, as an investor, this means that if one investment in the fund dips, the others might still be performing well, which can help buffer against losses.

Mutual funds are particularly appealing for new investors because they handle the heavy lifting. You don't need to research every stock or bond; the fund manager does that for you. Plus, because you're pooling resources with other investors, you can get started with relatively small amounts of money. It's a way to get a taste of a large, diversified portfolio without the hefty price tag or the hassle of managing it yourself.

ETFs for Beginners: The Flexible Investment

Exchange-Traded Funds (ETFs) are like mutual funds' trendy cousins. They also pool money from many investors to buy a diversified portfolio, but with a twist—they trade on stock exchanges, just like individual stocks. This means you can buy and sell shares of

ETFs throughout the trading day at market price. Imagine grabbing a plate from the potluck anytime you want, not just when the dinner starts or ends.

One of the biggest advantages of ETFs is their flexibility. Because they trade like stocks, you have more control over when you buy or sell, and you can often do it with lower investment fees than you'll have to pay on traditional mutual funds. It's an efficient way to diversify your investments and a fantastic tool for new investors who want both diversity and flexibility.

Choosing Investments for Your Goals: Aligning Your Financial Compass

When you're faced with the choice between bonds, mutual funds, and ETFs, how do you make the right decision? Start with your goals and timeline. If you're saving for a short-term goal, like a big trip in a couple of years, you might lean toward more stable investments like bonds or bond ETFs, which reduce the risk of major changes in value. For long-term goals like retirement, you might look toward mutual funds or stock ETFs, which can offer higher growth potential over time.

Also, consider your appetite for risk and how much time you want to spend managing your investments. If you prefer a set-it-and-forget-it approach, mutual funds managed by professionals can be a great choice. If you like having more control and the ability to make quick changes, ETFs might be more your style. If security is your top priority, traditional bonds can provide that steady, reliable investment you might be looking for.

As you navigate through these options, think of yourself as a chef in a well-stocked kitchen. Each ingredient—bonds, mutual funds, ETFs —has its role to play in your financial recipe. By understanding what each one brings to the table and how they align with your financial taste and goals, you can mix and match them to create a portfolio that's nutritious for your financial health and deliciously rewarding.

5.4 NAVIGATING CRYPTOCURRENCY: WHAT YOUNG ADULTS SHOULD KNOW

Cryptocurrency Basics: Diving into the Digital Coin Pool

Let's start by unpacking the enigma that is cryptocurrency, often just called crypto, because who isn't into a good nickname? Cryptocurrency is a type of digital money that only exists online. Unlike regular money, which banks and governments control, cryptocurrency is decentralized, meaning it's managed by a network of computers around the world. These computers use special technology called blockchain to keep track of all transactions. Think of blockchain as a digital notebook where every page records transactions. Once a page is full, it gets added to the end of the notebook, and everyone involved gets an identical copy of this notebook. Because each new page is connected to the previous one, and everyone has the same copy, it's almost impossible to change anything without everyone noticing. This makes blockchain a very secure way to keep track of transactions. With cryptocurrency, you can send and receive payments directly without needing a bank, and all transactions are secure and can't be changed once they're made. Transactions with cryptocurrencies like Bitcoin, Ethereum, or even those quirky Dogecoins are recorded on this blockchain, ensuring that they are secure and, once made, irreversible.

What really makes cryptocurrencies stand out in the crowded playground of financial options? It's their ability to cut out the middleman—no banks, no fees for transferring money, no waiting periods. It's like sending an email; you send your crypto directly to someone else, and—BOOM!—transaction completed. This simplicity and speed, combined with the allure of sometimes making hefty profits, have catapulted cryptocurrencies from a geeky niche to a significant player in the digital age economy.

Risks and Rewards: The Crypto Roller Coaster

Now, hold on to your hats because if you thought roller coasters at the amusement park were a thrill, the cryptocurrency market takes it to a new level. Prices can skyrocket, then plunge to knee-shaking lows, all within the time it takes to binge-watch your favorite series. The reasons? Everything from changes in market sentiment, technological advancements, regulatory news, or even tweets from high-profile individuals can sway prices dramatically.

The rewards can be tempting—stories of crypto millionaires who timed their investments right are enough to make anyone's ears perk up. However, for every success story, there are tales of those who faced significant losses. It's crucial to remember that investing in crypto should be more about strategy and less about following the hype. Think of it as a spice in your investment stew—not the main ingredient, but something you add thoughtfully to enhance your overall portfolio.

Safe Practices: Keeping Your Digital Wallet Secure

If you're ready to dip your toes in the crypto waters, how do you keep your investment safe? First, think about storage. Cryptocurrencies are stored in digital wallets, which can be online, on your computer, or even on a hardware device, almost resembling a USB drive. Each type has its pros and cons regarding security and ease of use. Online wallets are convenient but vulnerable to hacking. Hardware wallets, while less convenient for quick trading, offer an extra layer of security by keeping your crypto offline.

Next, consider the platforms you use for buying and trading crypto. Not all platforms are created equal. Look for ones with strong security measures, positive user reviews, and transparency. Ensure that they use two-factor authentication, which adds an additional layer of security beyond just a password. Always ensure you have strong, unique passwords for your accounts. It's like locking your car— taking a few extra seconds to ensure security can save a lot of headaches later.

Regulatory and Tax Implications: Navigating the Crypto Legal Landscape

Just because crypto operates independently of traditional banks doesn't mean it's a free-for-all. Governments are increasingly interested in regulating cryptocurrencies, which can impact their value, how they're traded, and what you need to report come tax time. Staying informed about the regulatory environment in your country is crucial. For instance, in the U.S., the IRS treats cryptocurrencies as property, not currency, meaning gains or losses from crypto transactions are subject to capital gains tax.

When it comes to taxes, it's essential to keep detailed records of your transactions, including dates, amounts, and what the transaction was for. This documentation will be invaluable when reporting your taxes and ensuring that you're compliant with the laws. Remember that the anonymity of crypto transactions doesn't mean they're invisible to tax authorities. As with any investment, being upfront and transparent is your best policy.

Navigating the world of cryptocurrencies can be as exciting as it is bewildering. With their potential for high returns comes a not-insignificant level of risk and a steep learning curve. By under-standing the basics, being aware of the risks, practicing secure investing habits, and staying informed about regulatory changes, you can better prepare yourself to make educated decisions in the crypto market. Whether you decide to invest or not, understanding this evolving landscape is becoming increasingly important in our digital world, offering insights into the future of your money but into the future of global finance itself.

5.5 RETIREMENT ACCOUNTS: NOT JUST FOR ADULTS

So, you think retirement is just for old folks? Think again! Starting to stash away some cash for your golden years while you're still in your golden youth can be one of the savviest financial moves you make. Why? One word: compounding. This magical finance wizardry allows your savings to grow exponentially over time as you earn interest on your interest. Think of it this way: the earlier you plant a tree, the longer it has to grow tall and strong.

Now, let's chat about the types of retirement accounts that can help you grow that mighty oak. There are IRAs (Individual Retirement Accounts) and employer-sponsored plans like 401(k)s. Choosing between them is a bit like picking your favorite ice cream flavor—each has its perks.

Traditional IRAs are like classic vanilla; you get tax deductions on your contributions now, which means you can lower your taxable income today, but you'll pay taxes when you withdraw the money in retirement. Roth IRAs? They're more like a reverse chocolate sundae; you pay taxes on your contributions now, but when you retire, you can make withdrawals tax-free. Sweet, right?

Then there's the 401(k), often offered through employers, which can feel like getting a double scoop. You contribute pre-tax income (lowering your taxable income now), and many employers will match a portion of your contributions. It's like getting free toppings on your sundae because who doesn't love free stuff? However, with 401(k)s, you'll pay taxes when you withdraw the money during retirement.

Navigating the limits and benefits of these accounts is essential. For 2024, you can contribute up to $6,500 a year to IRAs if you're under 50, and up to $22,500 a year to 401(K)s. These caps occasionally grow to account for inflation, like how your jeans might feel a bit tighter after Thanksgiving dinner, so you adjust the waistband. Staying within these limits while maximizing contributions can significantly impact the size of your retirement fund. Think of it as playing a financial Tetris; the better you fit your pieces within the limits, the clearer your path to a solid financial future.

Now, let's go on to automating your contributions because, let's be honest, remembering to transfer money every month is a hassle. Setting up an automatic transfer from your paycheck to your retirement account ensures that you consistently save without even thinking about it. Plus, it removes the temptation to spend what you might otherwise save. Out of sight, out of mind, right into your future pockets.

At 20, Emma decided to secure her financial future by opening a Roth IRA. Despite a modest income from her part-time job, she committed to contributing $200 a month, setting up automatic transfers to stay on track. She chose low-fee index funds for a diversified portfolio.

By starting early, Emma capitalized on compound interest. Contributing $200 monthly with an average annual return of 7%, she is projected to grow her savings to over $500,000 by age 60, from just $96,000 in contributions.

At 30, Mike decided to start saving for retirement. With a stable income, he committed to contributing $500 a month to a Roth IRA, setting up automatic transfers to stay disciplined. He chose low-fee index funds for a diversified portfolio. Starting later, Mike will miss out on some compound interest benefits. Contributing $500 monthly, with an average annual return of 7%, he is projected to grow his savings to over $400,000 by age 60, from $180,000 in contributions.

See the difference 10 years can make? Emma contributed $84,000 less than Mike, but her savings will grow to be over $100,000 more. Her early and disciplined approach to saving highlights the power of starting young and being consistent.

As we wrap up this chapter on the ins and outs of investing, from micro-investing to retirement planning, remember that investing is not just about growing your wealth. It's about creating opportunities for yourself and ensuring a secure and fulfilling future. Whether you're trading stocks, saving up in ETFs, or planning for retirement, each step builds greater financial independence.

ACTION CHECKLIST FOR BEGINNERS IN INVESTING

1. Start with Micro-Investing

- Choose a Micro-Investing Platform: Find one with low fees and user-friendly features.
- Set Up Automatic Round-Ups: Enable round-up features to invest spare change from everyday purchases.
- Start Small: Begin with small amounts to build the habit of investing.

2. Automate Your Investments

- Set Up Automatic Transfers: Arrange for regular transfers to your investment account (weekly, biweekly, or monthly).
- Use Dollar-Cost Averaging: Invest a fixed amount at regular intervals to mitigate market volatility.

3. Understand Risk and Return

- **Assess Your Risk Tolerance**: Determine how much risk you can handle based on your financial goals.
- **Diversify Your Investments**: Spread your money across different assets to minimize risk.

4. Set Clear Investment Goals

- Define Short-Term and Long-Term Goals: Identify what you're investing for and the timeline.
- Align Investments with Goals: Choose investments that match your risk tolerance and timeline for each goal.

5. Educate Yourself on Different Investment Types

- Learn About Bonds: Understand their role as stable, interest-earning investments.
- Explore Mutual Funds and ETFs: Consider these for diversification and professional management.
- Understand the Stock Market: Learn how to read stock charts and the importance of diversification.

6. Stay Consistent and Patient

- Regularly Review Your Portfolio: Monitor your investments and make adjustments as needed.
- Stick to Your Plan: Keep investing regularly, regardless of market conditions.

7. Secure Your Investments

- Use Secure Platforms: Ensure that your investment platform has strong security measures.
- Keep Records: Maintain detailed records of your investments for tax purposes.

CHAPTER 6
EARNING MORE

Never spend money before you have earned it.

THOMAS JEFFERSON

Managing the money you have is crucial, but increasing your earnings can go a long way as you strive to attain true financial independence. This chapter will guide you through practical strategies to boost your income, from landing your first job to navigating the gig economy and turning hobbies into profitable ventures. By applying these techniques, you can achieve financial stability and pave the way for future success. Whether you're just starting out or looking to diversify your income streams, this chapter offers actionable insights to help you earn more and reach your financial goals.

6.1 PROVEN TECHNIQUES FOR JOB HUNTING SUCCESS: A PRACTICAL GUIDE

Finding employment as a teen or young adult can be an exciting yet challenging experience. It's an important and necessary part of growing into the next phase of life, but it takes some effort on your part. Start by crafting a solid resume—consider it your personal highlight reel. Even if you don't have much work experience, you can spotlight volunteer work, school projects, and extracurricular activities. Skills like teamwork, communication, and problem-solving are your star players here. Keep your resume concise, professional, and tailored to each job you're applying for.

Next up is networking. Don't underestimate the power of personal connections. Talk to family, friends, teachers, and community members about your job search. They might know about hidden job opportunities that aren't listed online. Volunteering and internships are also excellent ways to build your network and gain valuable experience that can lead to job offers.

Preparing for interviews is another important step. Practice answering common interview questions and developing clear, concise responses highlighting your skills and experiences. Dress the part, show up on time, and bring your A-game with positive body language and good communication skills. Think of it like playing a role in a performance—posture, eye contact, and active listening are key to making a great impression.

Being proactive and persistent is also vital. Apply to multiple job listings, and follow up with employers after you submit your applications. Showing genuine interest and enthusiasm can set you apart from the crowd. Explore various types of employment, such as part-time jobs, seasonal work, and freelance opportunities. These positions can provide valuable experience and help you build a solid work ethic.

Finally, never stop learning. Take advantage of online courses, workshops, and certifications related to your field of interest. Continuous learning shows potential employers that you're dedicated and eager to grow. By following these best practices, teens and young adults can boost their chances of landing meaningful employment and can lay the groundwork for a successful career.

Of course, everyone dreams of having a fulfilling job that they love, but this phase of life is the time to get experience, pay your bills, and focus on gaining the education or career training needed to reach your future goals. You might not love your job today, but it's a stepping stone to help you build the skills and financial stability needed for tomorrow's opportunities. Embrace this phase as a necessary part of your journey, knowing that each experience brings you closer to your desired career and life.

The Impact of Social Media on Your Future

In today's digital age, your social media presence is more than just a way to connect with friends and share your experiences; it's also a window into your character for prospective employers, landlords, admissions committees, and others. These individuals often look at your social media profiles to get a sense of who you are beyond your resume or application. This practice can significantly impact your opportunities, so it's essential to manage your online presence carefully.

Employers use social media to screen candidates before making hiring decisions. They look for red flags such as inappropriate content, discriminatory comments, or any behavior that might suggest a lack of professionalism. Posts that show poor judgment, such as excessive partying or illegal activities, can make employers question your reliability and integrity. On the other hand, positive posts about volunteer work, academic achievements, and other constructive activities can enhance your appeal, showing that you are responsible and well-rounded.

Landlords also use social media to evaluate potential tenants. They are looking for responsible individuals who will take care of their property and be good neighbors. It's important to present yourself as someone who respects others and maintains a stable lifestyle.

College admissions officers often check applicants' profiles to gain insights into their character, leadership, and extracurricular activities. Internship coordinators look for professionalism and alignment with company culture. Volunteer organizations ensure potential volunteers align with their mission and values. Loan officers and financial institutions may assess an applicant's stability and reliability through their online presence. Professional licensing boards review social media to ensure candidates meet ethical and professional standards. Athletic programs and professional sports teams scrutinize profiles to evaluate behavior, attitude, and suitability for the team's culture. Government agencies, especially for security clearances or government jobs, conduct thorough social media reviews to assess an individual's reliability and trustworthiness.

By being aware of who might be viewing your social media, you can take steps to present yourself in a positive and professional light, enhancing your chances of success in various applications.

6.2 THE GIG ECONOMY AND YOU: OPPORTUNITIES AND RISKS

Fortunately, there are more ways than ever to earn money in today's world, and the gig economy might just be the sidekick your wallet needs. The gig economy is a vibrant universe where short-term tasks, freelance assignments, and temporary contracts thrive. It's like the Wild West of the job market, offering freedom, flexibility, and a fistful of dollars for those ready to hustle.

Understanding the Gig Economy: More Than Just a Buzzword

So, what's the gig economy really about? Imagine a marketplace buzzing like a downtown bazaar, where skills meet opportunities in a flurry of transactions. This economic model is fueled by freelance jobs, project-based work, and temporary contracts—think driving for Uber, designing graphics on a per-project basis, or coding up a storm for a startup over a weekend. What makes the gig economy tick is its flexibility; it allows you to work when you want, how you want, and as much as you want. It's tailored for the Netflix generation—on-demand and highly personalized.

Finding Gig Work: Your Gateway to Flexibility

Ready to dive in? Finding gig work that suits your skills can be as exciting as shopping for those perfect, not-too-tight, not-too-baggy jeans. Start by taking inventory of what you can do and what you enjoy. Can you write catchy content, design sleek websites, or capture stunning photos? Platforms like *Upwork*, *Fiverr*, and *TaskRabbit* are the shopping malls for gig work, where you can pick and choose opportunities that fit your style. Set up a profile, showcase your skills, and browse the gigs. It's like online dating, but instead of finding your soul mate, you match with the perfect job.

Exploring Online Platforms: The Digital Storefronts

Platforms such as *Upwork*, *Fiverr*, and *Etsy* serve as your launchpad. They're similar to those trendy pop-up stores in the city, except that they pop up right on your screen. *Upwork* is great for a wide range of freelance work—from writing and graphic design to web development and marketing. *Fiverr* offers gigs that start at $5 (hence the name), perfect for smaller tasks or building up your portfolio. *Etsy* is the go-to for selling anything handcrafted—from knitted scarves to hand-painted mugs. These platforms connect you to clients and handle the payment and feedback details, letting you focus on what you do best.

Building a Strong Profile: Your Digital Handshake

Think of your online profile as your professional handshake—strong, confident, and promising quality. Here's the twist: you're not there in person, so your profile needs to sing your praises for you. Start with a professional photo—yes, ditch the beach selfie. Write a clear, concise description of your skills and what you bring to the table. Include a portfolio of your best work—your personal highlight reel. Customer reviews can be pure gold. Encourage clients to leave feedback—it's word-of-mouth for the digital age.

Networking and Building Relationships: Beyond the Screen

While the gig economy might seem like a solo journey, it's really a bustling network of professionals just like you. Building relationships is important. Connect with other freelancers, join online forums, and participate in community discussions. Platforms like LinkedIn can be great for this. It's like mingling at a party, except everyone's potentially your next client or collaborator. The stronger your network, the more likely you are to land gigs regularly.

Managing Gig Income: Not Just Pocket Change

Here comes the tricky part—managing your gig income. Unlike a steady paycheck, gig work can fluctuate, making budgeting feel like a game of whack-a-mole. First, track all of your income and expenses diligently. Consider setting aside a portion of each gig payment for taxes (yes, Uncle Sam will want a piece of your pie). Here's a pro tip: funnel some of your earnings into an emergency fund. It's your financial backup plan, providing a cushion for slower months.

Navigating Risks: The Safety Nets

The gig economy isn't without its pitfalls. Job insecurity and the lack of benefits—like health insurance or a retirement plan—are real concerns. Mitigate these risks by diversifying your gig sources so all your income eggs aren't in one basket. Look into freelance unions or groups that offer member benefits, including health insurance. Always read the fine print on gig contracts to know what you're getting into and protect your rights.

Navigating the gig economy is like mastering a new game. The rules are different, the pace is faster, and the rewards—while potentially greater—come with their own set of challenges. Even so, with a bit of savvy, a dash of caution, and a whole lot of hustle, the gig economy can not just supplement your income but might even revamp your career. Just remember, in this game, flexibility is your best friend, and your ability to adapt is your ace in the hole. Ready to play?

6.3 FROM PASSION TO PROFIT: TURNING HOBBIES INTO CASH

Imagine that your weekend dabbling in painting, coding, or even gardening could actually fatten your wallet. Transforming hobbies into a source of income is not just for the lucky few; it's a real possibility for anyone willing to channel their passion into profit. The secret sauce? Recognizing which of your hobbies has market potential and understanding how to monetize it effectively.

First up, identify your marketable hobbies. Consider what you love doing so much that you lose track of time—maybe it's creating digital art, baking cupcakes, or making handmade jewelry. Now, ask yourself, "Would someone pay for this?" If you often get compliments or requests from friends or family for your creations, that's a green light. Dive deeper by researching online. Check out forums, social media, and marketplaces to see if there's a demand for your hobby. For instance, if you're into knitting, a quick search on *Etsy* or *Pinterest* can reveal how much people are willing to pay for hand-knitted scarves or beanies. You want to find a niche that both excites you and appeals to potential customers.

Now, where to showcase your newfound business? The platform you choose can make a big difference. If your hobby involves creating tangible goods like artwork or crafts, *Etsy* is great for selling handmade items. It's user-friendly and boasts a large audience specifically looking for unique, handcrafted products. For digital services like graphic design or video editing, platforms like YouTube can be a medium to showcase your skills and earn through ad revenue and sponsorships. Let's not forget about Instagram, which is perfect for visually-oriented hobbies like photography or food art. It provides a global stage to display your work and to attract customers through engaging posts and stories.

Pricing your work can be as tricky as being a cat on a skateboard. You need to find that sweet spot where customers feel they're getting value and you feel fairly compensated for your time and skill. Start by researching what others in the market charge for similar products or services. Don't just go with the lowest price— consider the quality and uniqueness of what you offer. A good strategy is to calculate your costs (materials, time, overhead) and add a profit margin that feels right. Remember that you must cover costs while valuing your creativity and effort.

Marketing doesn't have to mean putting on a suit and playing buzzword bingo. At its core, it's about connecting with people who might love your work. Start by telling your story. Why do you create what you do? What's special about it? Use your social media platforms to share these stories, along with high-quality images or videos of your products or behind-the-scenes peeks into your creative process. Engage with your followers by responding to comments, asking questions, and even running small contests. This builds a community around your brand, turning casual viewers into loyal customers.

Customer engagement is the cherry on top. Making a sale is great, but you also want to create an experience that keeps people coming back. Include personalized thank-you notes in your orders, offer special discounts to repeat customers, or keep them updated with exciting developments through newsletters. When customers feel valued, they're not only more likely to buy again but also to spread the word. In today's digital age, a happy customer can be your best marketing tool, sharing their positive experiences and thus drawing a broader audience to your offerings.

By transforming your hobby into a profitable venture, you're earning extra cash and enriching your life by doing what you love. It's about leveraging your natural talents and passions, turning them into an enterprise that brings joy not just to you but also to your customers. So, take that hobby off the back burner and turn it into something amazing, one step at a time.

6.4 BALANCING SIDE HUSTLES WITH SCHOOL AND/OR WORK

Imagine you're a circus juggler, but instead of colorful balls, you're keeping school, a job, and a side hustle in the air. Here's the twist— none of those balls can afford to drop. This is the reality for many hustlers who are grinding to make ends meet, save for a dream, or fund their next big adventure. Balancing this trifecta requires some serious skills in time management, boundary setting, productivity, and a clear-eyed view of what each gig really adds to your life.

Let's kick off with time management, your secret weapon in the war against the clock. Effective time management is about prioritizing and giving each aspect of your life its due without burning the midnight oil too often. Start with the basics: get yourself a planner or use a digital calendar. Block out times for school, work, and side hustles, but also carve out time for rest, exercise, and a bit of fun. Create a rhythm that keeps you engaged but not overwhelmed. Check out systems like the Pomodoro Technique, in which you work in focused bursts followed by short breaks, which can dramatically increase your productivity without leading to burnout. Remember that the goal is to run a marathon, not a sprint—your pace needs to sustain you long-term.

Now, on to setting boundaries—your defense mechanism against the world's demands. It's easy to say yes to every project, every shift, or every request, but at what cost? Setting clear boundaries involves knowing when to say no, and that's a powerful skill. It recognizes when a gig is pulling too much from your energy reserves and threatens to tip your work-life balance into the red. Communicate your availability clearly to your employers or clients, stick to it, and guard your off-time zealously. Respect your own limits and ensure that others do the same. Your time and energy aren't infinite resources, and managing them wisely sometimes means guarding the gates.

Maximizing productivity is where you get to shine. Work smarter, not harder. Tools and apps can be lifesavers here. Use task management apps like *Asana* or *Trello* to keep track of your projects and deadlines. Automate where possible—set up email filters, use accounting software to track gig earnings, or schedule social media posts using tools like *Buffer*. Each little efficiency adds up, freeing you to focus on the work itself rather than on the administration of the work. Additionally, create a conducive work environment. A dedicated workspace, whether it's a desk in your bedroom or a spot at the local café, can signal to your brain that it's time to focus, increasing your output and decreasing the time it takes to get your tasks done.

Finally, evaluating the worth of your side hustle is crucial. Not all gigs are created equal. Some might offer more money; others might offer more satisfaction or skill-building opportunities. Regularly assess whether your side hustles align with your financial goals and personal values. Are they worth the time and energy you're investing? If a hustle isn't meeting your expectations, it might be time to reconsider or replace it. This evaluation isn't only about monetary gain; it's about ensuring that your side hustles enrich your life, not detract from it.

Managing the balancing act of school, work, and side hustles is no small feat. It requires a clear strategy, disciplined time management, firm boundaries, and constant evaluation to ensure alignment with your goals. As you move forward, keep these tools in your arsenal, and you'll not only survive the juggling act but also thrive, making each component of your busy life work for you, not against you.

As we wrap up this chapter on maximizing your earning potential through side hustles, remember the key takeaways: manage your time like a pro, set and respect your boundaries to avoid burnout, boost your productivity with smart tools and habits, and regularly evaluate the contribution of your side gigs to your financial and personal growth. These strategies will ensure that your side hustles are a beneficial addition to your life, complementing your main commitments and helping you build toward your goals.

ACTION STEPS FOR EARNING MORE

1. Create a Strong Resume:

- Highlight volunteer work, school projects, and key skills.
- Keep it concise and tailored to each job.

2. Network Effectively:

- Use personal connections and internships to find job opportunities.

3. Prepare for Interviews:

- Practice common questions, and use positive body language.

4. Explore the Gig Economy:

- Use platforms like *Upwork*, *Fiverr*, and *TaskRabbit* to find freelance work.
- Build a strong online profile and manage gig income responsibly.

5. Turn Hobbies into Cash:

- Identify marketable hobbies and use platforms like *Etsy* and Instagram to sell.
- Engage customers with personalized touches and good marketing.

CHAPTER 7
TAXES 101

" *In this world, nothing can be said to be certain, except death and taxes.*

BENJAMIN FRANKLIN

Imagine that it's payday and you're ready to buy all of your essentials, add to your emergency fund and have a little bit of fun, but when you get your hands on your paycheck, the numbers seem to have played a cruel game of shrinkage. Where did all that money go? And who is FICA? Welcome to the world of taxes and withholdings, the villains of your paycheck drama. Let's look at that pay stub, decode those deductions, and maybe even find a way to keep a bit more of your money when the next payday rolls around.

7.1 UNDERSTANDING YOUR PAYCHECK: TAXES EXPLAINED

Deciphering Your Pay Stub: Breaking Down the Various Deductions and What They Mean

First up is that pay stub. At first glance, you'll see your gross income, which is your salary, before any deductions or taxes. Then comes the not-so-fun part—deductions. These might include federal and state taxes, Social Security, Medicare, and possibly a slew of others, depending on where you live and work. Each deduction takes a piece of your paycheck before it hits your bank account.

First up is a payroll tax called FICA (Federal Insurance Contributions Act), which is used to fund Social Security and Medicare. It is pretty straightforward: they fund your future self's retirement days and medical needs. But federal and state taxes? They're like a subscription fee for living and working in your country and state—they pay for roads, schools, emergency services, and more. Your pay stub likely shows both the amount taken out for this pay period and the total for the year, which can be helpful come tax time or for financial planning.

Federal vs. State Taxes

On to the battle of the taxes: federal vs. state. Everyone pays federal taxes, which go into the nation's big money pot to fund nationwide programs and services. But state taxes? They're the wildcard. Depending on where you live, you might pay high state taxes, no state taxes, or something in between. States like Texas and Florida boast a no-state-income-tax policy, giving residents a bit more leeway in their personal budgets. Others, like California and New York, take a more significant bite. Understanding this can dramatically affect your take-home pay and might even influence future decisions about where you live and work.

Common Tax Terms Explained

We've touched on gross income—your salary before all the deductions, but what about net income? That's your take-home pay after all those hungry little deductions have had their fill. If gross income is your pie in the sky, net income is the pie you actually get to eat. Withholdings are how much of your pie is set aside for taxes during each pay period. It's a forced savings account for your tax bill; saving gradually is better than being hit with a huge bill at once.

Adjusting Your Withholdings: How to Ensure You're Not Overpaying or Underpaying Taxes Throughout the Year

Speaking of withholdings, did you know you can adjust these? If you typically get a huge tax refund, you might be overdoing it on withholdings, giving the government a free loan from your paycheck. Conversely, if you end up owing a lot at tax time, you might need to withhold more. Adjusting your withholdings can help keep your paycheck and tax liabilities in balance. It's like tuning your guitar to make sure it's pitch-perfect for your next concert—get the withholdings right, and your financial tune sounds sweet all year long.

Changing the tax withholdings from your paycheck typically involves updating your tax withholdings form(s) with your employer. Here are the general steps you can follow:

1. Obtain the Correct Form(s): In the U.S., this is the IRS Form W-4. Other countries may have similar forms for adjusting federal tax withholdings. In the U.S., there may also be a parallel form for your state.

2. Fill Out the Form:

- **Personal Information**: Provide your name, address, Social Security number, and marital status.
- **Multiple Jobs**: If you have more than one job, you might need to account for additional withholding.
- **Other Adjustments**: You can specify other income, deductions, and extra withholding amounts as needed.

3. Submit the Form: Once filled out, submit the form to your employer's HR or payroll department. Some employers have an online system for updating your W-4 electronically.

4. Review Paychecks: After submitting the form, review your subsequent paychecks to ensure that the withholdings changes have been correctly implemented.

5. Re-evaluate Periodically: It's a good idea to re-evaluate your withholdings periodically, especially if you experience life changes or changes in income.

Refer to the form's instructions for detailed instructions, or consult a tax professional if you're unsure how to fill it out.

Navigating the intricacies of your paycheck and understanding where your money goes can empower you to make smarter financial decisions. We would all love to keep a bit more of that hard-earned cash to enjoy right now. Who knows? With a little tweaking, your emergency fund may get a little bigger, no magic required—just a better understanding of your taxes and withholdings.

7.2 FILING YOUR TAXES: A STEP-BY-STEP GUIDE

Preparation Is Key: The documents and information you need to gather before you start the filing process

Okay, so it's tax season again—the time of year when adulting hits hard and all that paperwork you've shoved in a drawer comes back to haunt you. But fear not! With a bit of prep, you can tackle your taxes like a boss. First things first. Let's talk about gathering your documents. This is like prepping for a big project. Having all your materials at hand makes the process way smoother. You'll need:

- W-2 forms from employers
- 1099 forms if you've done freelance work
- Interest statements from banks if you've got savings or investment accounts.
- Have you paid tuition or student loan interest? Grab those forms too (1098-E for student loan interest and 1098-T for tuition statements).
- If you've made any charitable donations, those receipts are golden for possible deductions.

Choosing the Right Filing Status: How to choose the one that gives you the best tax advantages

Now, let's navigate the maze of filing statuses. Your filing status is a key player in the tax game—it affects your filing requirements, standard deduction amounts, and eligibility for certain credits and deductions. The main statuses are Single, Married Filing Jointly, Married Filing Separately, Head of Household, and Qualifying Widow(er) with Dependent Child. Single is pretty straightforward—

if you're not married, this is likely you. Married Filing Jointly often results in lower taxes and higher deductions, but if you and your spouse prefer to keep your finances separate, or if one of you has significant medical expenses, filing separately might be the way to go. Head of Household is for unmarried folks who pay more than half the cost of keeping up a home for themselves and a qualifying person (like a child or parent). Lastly, if your spouse has passed away and you have a dependent child, you might qualify as a Qualifying Widow(er), which allows you to use joint return tax rates and the highest standard deduction for up to two years after the death. Choose wisely; the right status can significantly impact your tax situation.

Navigating Tax Forms: The most common tax forms, such as the W-2, 1099, and 1040

Feeling overwhelmed by tax forms? Let's take a look at the main characters in this drama. The W-2 form is pretty much your employment summary—how much you earned and what was taken out for taxes. It's your financial report card from your employer. Then there's the 1099 form, the freelancers' companion—it reports income from freelance work, dividends, or interest. Now, the star of the show: the 1040 form. This is where you summarize your entire year—income, deductions, credits—and finally, get to see how much you owe or get back. It's like the final exam, where you show your work and figure out your grade (in this case, your tax refund or liability).

Filing Methods: Pros and cons of different filing methods

When it comes to filing your taxes, you've got options. Old school paper filing is like handwriting your term paper—it's reliable, but it can be slow, and the risk of mistakes is higher. Enter tax software, the modern solution that's like using a word processor with spell check

—it makes everything easier and faster, often with step-by-step guidance and calculations that reduce errors. Additionally, e-filing through software generally means a quicker refund. But what if your tax situation is complex, or you just really don't want to deal with it? That's when a tax professional comes in handy. Think of them as a tutor who can help you navigate complex problems and ensure that everything is correct. Sure, it costs more, but for peace of mind and potentially maximized deductions, it can be well worth it.

Common Filing Mistakes: Common errors to avoid when filing your taxes

Finally, let's talk about common pitfalls. Common mistakes include incorrect social security numbers, forgetting to sign your return or missing deadlines—all of which can lead to delays or penalties. Double-check every entry, especially your personal info. Another biggie is not reporting all your income. Remember those 1099s? Yeah, the IRS (Internal Revenue Service) gets copies, too, so make sure everything matches up. Don't forget that deductions and credits are like bonus points that can lower your tax bill. Just make sure you have records to back them up because if the IRS calls you out, you'll need to show your work.

The IRS enforces tax laws by conducting audits (detailed examinations of individual tax returns to ensure accuracy and compliance with tax laws), investigating tax fraud and evasion, assessing penalties and interest on unpaid taxes, and taking legal action such as liens and levies to collect outstanding tax debts. A tax lien is when the government places a legal claim on your property because you didn't pay your taxes. The government can take your stuff, like your car or house, if you don't pay what you owe. A tax levy is a legal action to seize a taxpayer's assets to satisfy unpaid tax debts. This can include taking money directly from your bank account or "garnishing wages," which means the government can take money from your paycheck before you even get your hands on it. In short, always be accurate and honest with your taxes because the IRS will eventually find you if you don't, and it won't be a pleasant experience.

7.3 TAX DEDUCTIONS AND CREDITS FOR YOUNG ADULTS

Let's dive into tax deductions and credits, shall we? Think of these as the cheat codes of the tax world—they can seriously level up your tax return game, reducing how much you owe or boosting that sweet refund. First, a quick breakdown: deductions lower your taxable income (that's the amount of your income that's subject to taxes), while credits give you a dollar-for-dollar reduction on your actual tax bill. So, if deductions are like getting a discount when you buy a space rocket (because who doesn't dream a bit big?), credits are more like getting a rebate check after you've bought it.

Now, onto some gold nuggets you might not know about, specifically tailored for you, the young adults stepping into this fiscal jungle. We'll start with education expenses and student loan interest since education costs more than just a few pretty pennies these days. If you're currently paying off student loans, the IRS might be kinder than you think. You could deduct up to $2,500 of the interest you paid on your student loans over the year. Yes, that's money you can subtract directly from your taxable income, which might help take the sting out of those monthly payments. Just remember that there are income limits that might phase out this deduction, so if you've landed a particularly lucrative gig, double-check to see if you still qualify.

There's more on the education front. Credits like the American Opportunity Credit (AOC) can be a game-changer. This gem offers up to $2,500 per student per year for the first four years of college.

Expenses that count toward this credit aren't just tuition; they also include books, supplies, and equipment. However, there's a plot twist—40% of it is refundable, which means if the credit drops your tax liability to zero, you could get up to $1,000 back. Let's not forget its cousin, the Lifetime Learning Credit, which offers up to $2,000 per tax return (not per student) and doesn't require a minimum course load, making it perfect if you're taking career development classes or pursuing graduate studies part-time.

Maximizing these deductions and credits involves a bit of strategy. First, keep impeccable records. Every form, receipt, or document related to educational expenses should be filed and ready to whip out if needed. Don't just shove them in a shoebox under your bed. Organize them in a way that would make Marie Kondo proud. Next, if you're juggling school and a side hustle, make sure to explore every possible credit or deduction related to both. Sometimes, educational expenses can overlap with business expenses, especially if your studies directly relate to your business. This overlap can sometimes offer double the deductions if navigated correctly.

Navigating the nuances of these tax benefits might seem daunting, but understanding them can lead to significant savings. Armed with this knowledge, you can approach your taxes with a newfound confidence, ready to claim every credit and deduction you rightfully deserve. With each tax season, you'll get better at spotting and maximizing these opportunities, turning what was once a bewildering chore into a rewarding annual ritual. So, gear up, get your documents in order, and remember: in the game of taxes, knowledge is not just power—it's money.

7.4 GIG WORK AND TAXES: WHAT YOU NEED TO KNOW

Let's face it: the gig economy isn't just a buzzword—it's your late-night Uber rides, your weekend photo shoots, and those graphic design gigs that keep your creativity buzzing. But when it comes to taxes, gig work can feel like stepping onto a roller coaster that's missing a few crucial signs. Are you strapped in and ready? Let's look at the tax maze that every gig worker needs to navigate.

Self-Employment Tax Responsibilities: Navigating the Waters of Gig Economy Taxes

First up are self-employment taxes. If you've ever wondered why your musician friend keeps mumbling about self-employment taxes, here's the scoop. When you work a regular 9-to-5, your employer handles your Social Security and Medicare taxes, neatly deducting them from your paycheck. However, in the realm of gig work, you are the boss, and the taxman expects you to handle this on your own. This means paying both the employee's and the employer's share of Social Security and Medicare, which totals up to approximately 15.3% of your net earnings. Sounds hefty, right? It's like finding out your free streaming service trial has ended, and now you've got to pay up if you want to keep binge-watching.

Now, to prevent an end-of-year tax horror show, the IRS wants its cut quarterly. That's right; quarterly estimated tax payments are your new season tickets to the gig worker's tax game. Mark your calendar for mid-April, June, September, and January. Missing these dates can lead to penalties, kind of like racking up late fees at a library, except these books cost a lot more. To figure out how much to pay, you'll need to estimate your yearly earnings and calculate the corresponding taxes. It's a bit like trying to guess how many jellybeans are in a jar.

Get it close, and you're golden. Way off? You might either owe a lump sum at tax time or get a refund.

Tracking Expenses: The Art of Keeping Meticulous Records

On to tracking expenses, which is less about hoarding every receipt and more about strategic saving. Every mile you drive, every lens you buy, and every cup of tea you sip while sketching out client designs could save you money on taxes. Why? Because these can be deductible expenses. To make sure you can take full advantage of deductible expenses, keep a detailed log of your income and expenses. Apps like *QuickBooks* or *Expensify* can turn this task into a breeze, categorizing your expenses and even tracking mileage through your phone's GPS. If you prefer a free method, just keep a folder handy and put your receipts in this folder throughout the year. Everything will be in one place and ready to go when tax time rolls around.

Here's a pro tip: not all expenses are created equal. Some are fully deductible, like advertising costs, while others, like meals, are only 50% deductible. Knowing the difference can be as crucial as knowing which wire to cut in a movie bomb-disposal scene—stressful, but with practice, you get better at making the right call.

As a teen or young adult working in the gig economy, there are several important tax deductions you can take advantage of to reduce your tax liability. Here are some key deductions to consider:

1. **Home office deduction**: If you use a portion of your home exclusively and regularly for your gig work, you can deduct a percentage of your rent, utilities, and other home-related expenses. To qualify, the space must be used solely for business purposes.
2. **Vehicle expenses:** If you use your car for gig work (e.g., rideshare driving), you can deduct either the actual

expenses or use the standard mileage rate. This includes costs like gas, insurance, and maintenance related to business use.

3. **Cell phone and internet:** You can deduct the portion of your cell phone bill and internet costs that are used for business purposes.

4. **Equipment and supplies:** Any equipment, tools, or supplies purchased specifically for your gig work are deductible. This could include laptops, printers, software subscriptions, or other job-specific items.

5. **Self-employment tax deduction:** You can deduct half of your self-employment tax, which covers Social Security and Medicare contributions.

6. **Health insurance premiums:** If you're self-employed and pay for your own health insurance, you may be able to deduct these premiums.

7. **Professional development:** Costs related to work-related education, training, or certifications can be deductible.

8. **Travel expenses:** If your gig work requires travel, you can deduct transportation, lodging, and meal costs (meals are typically 50% deductible, but were temporarily 100% deductible for 2021 and 2022).

9. **Advertising and marketing:** Expenses related to promoting your gig work, such as business cards or online ads, are deductible.

10. **Retirement contributions:** Contributions to self-employed retirement plans like SEP IRAs or Solo 401(k)s can be deductible.

It's crucial to keep detailed records of all your business-related expenses and income throughout the year. This will make it easier to claim deductions accurately when filing your taxes. Remember, you may need to make quarterly estimated tax payments to avoid penalties, as taxes are not automatically withheld from gig economy earnings.

Tax laws can change, and individual situations vary. It's always a good idea to consult with a qualified tax professional to ensure you're taking all the deductions you're entitled to and complying with tax regulations.

Form 1099-NEC: Understanding Your Gig Income Documentation

Enter Form 1099-NEC, the document that reports how much you've earned from each client who's paid you $600 or more during the year. No W-2s here—just a straightforward statement of what you've earned. What if a client ghosts you come tax season and doesn't send this form? First, don't panic. You should still report all your income, form or no form. Keep your own detailed records and invoices as proof of income because, unlike those mythical monsters under your bed, the IRS is very real and doesn't take kindly to unreported earnings.

Tax Tips for Gig Workers: Avoiding Common Pitfalls

Lastly, let's share some insider tax tips to keep you safe in the gig economy tax jungle. Always set aside a portion of each payment for taxes. Use a separate bank account for gig work to keep personal and professional finances distinct, which makes tracking and reporting much easier. Consider investing in a good accountant who understands self-employment nuances, especially if your gig work crosses into different tax categories or involves significant expenses.

Navigating taxes as a gig worker doesn't have to be a trip through a haunted house filled with surprises and scares. With the right tools, a bit of knowledge, and a proactive approach, you can turn this part of your gig life into a well-oiled machine—efficient, less terrifying, and maybe even rewarding. Keep your records straight, your estimates accurate, and your deadlines marked, and you'll master the art of gig economy taxes with the finesse of a seasoned pro.

7.5 SCHOLARSHIPS, GRANTS, AND TAXES: KEEPING IT STRAIGHT

Navigating the maze of scholarships and grants is like playing a game where the rules keep changing depending on whether you're using the funds for tuition or splurging on your dorm room pizza parties. Let's get this straight: not all scholarships and grants are created equal —at least, not in the eyes of the taxman. Generally, if you're using the money to pay for tuition, fees, books, and supplies directly required for your coursework, the IRS gives you a thumbs up—these aren't considered taxable income. However, if you use any part of that money for other expenses, like room and board or travel, it starts looking more like taxable income. Think of it as your scholarship going undercover—as long as it sticks to tuition and required supplies, it remains incognito from taxes.

Now, if you find yourself with scholarship or grant money that covers more than just the tuition costs, you'll need to report the extra as income. This often feels like discovering a plot twist in your favorite series—surprising, maybe a bit disappointing, but definitely something you need to handle. Reporting additional scholarship income is crucial because, just like any plot twist, ignoring it doesn't make it go away, and this could lead to complications later. When filing your tax return, this extra income needs to be included under the wages section, and yes, you'll need to pay taxes on it. It's like paying your dues for using that money on life's little extras outside your direct education costs.

Planning for Tax Implications: Strategize to Avoid End-of-Year Surprises

Planning for the tax implications of receiving scholarships or grants is like setting up chess pieces in a strategic game—the goal is to avoid checkmate when tax season rolls around. Start by understanding the full scope of how your scholarships or grants are allocated—how much is covering tuition and fees directly related to your coursework versus other expenses? Keeping detailed records throughout the year can save you a lot of headaches. Documentation is your ally, providing evidence if the IRS questions your tax return.

Moreover, consider how your scholarship impacts your eligibility for other tax credits and deductions. Sometimes, the tax benefits of declaring a portion of your scholarship as income (and thus paying taxes on it) might be outweighed by the larger deductions or credits you can claim. It's a balancing act, requiring a bit of math and maybe some professional advice to navigate effectively. Don't shy away from consulting a tax professional if things get complicated. They can help you get the best possible tax outcome.

Navigating the interplay among scholarships, grants, and taxes doesn't have to be a solo expedition fraught with uncertainty. With the right knowledge and strategies, you can manage your educational finances like a pro, maximizing benefits while staying compliant with tax laws. By understanding the tax implications of your scholarships and grants, and by making smart use of educational tax benefits, you're not just surviving the academic world; you're thriving financially within it.

Jane, a young graduate student balancing her studies with a part-time job, decided to learn about the intricacies of student tax credits to optimize her finances. By carefully documenting her tuition payments, textbook purchases, and school supplies, she was able to claim the American Opportunity Credit, which offered her up to $2,500 per year. Additionally, she deducted the interest on her student loans, reducing her taxable income further. This strategic use of tax credits and deductions not only minimized her tax liability but also resulted in a significant refund, easing the financial burden of her education and allowing her to save more for her future goals.

As this chapter closes, remember the importance of being proactive about your tax situation, especially when it comes to managing scholarships and grants. The knowledge you've gained here is more than just academic—it's a practical toolkit that will help you confidently navigate the complexities of taxes.

ACTION CHECKLIST FOR MANAGING YOUR TAXES

1. Understanding Your Paycheck: Taxes Explained

- Decipher Your Pay Stub: Understand the various deductions such as federal and state taxes, Social Security, and Medicare.
- Know the Difference: Differentiate between federal and state taxes and their impacts on your take-home pay.
- Familiarize Yourself with Terms: Learn key tax terms like gross income, net income, and withholdings.
- Adjust Withholdings: Use IRS Form W-4 to adjust your withholdings to avoid overpaying or underpaying taxes.

2. Filing Your Taxes: A Step-by-Step Guide

- Gather Documents: Collect necessary documents such as W-2s, 1099s, interest statements, and receipts for deductions.

- Choose Filing Status: Select the appropriate filing status (Single, Married Filing Jointly, etc.) for optimal tax advantages.
- Understand Common Tax Forms: Know the purposes of W-2, 1099, and 1040 forms.
- Decide on Filing Method: Choose between paper filing, tax software, or professional help based on your needs.
- Avoid Common Mistakes: Double-check entries, report all income, and meet deadlines to avoid penalties.

3. Tax Deductions and Credits for Young Adults

- Maximize Education Benefits: Utilize deductions for student loan interest, and credits like the American Opportunity Credit and the Lifetime Learning Credit.
- Keep Detailed Records: Maintain organized records of all educational expenses and related documents.
- Strategize Deductions: Explore overlapping deductions for education and business expenses if applicable.

4. Gig Work and Taxes: What You Need to Know

- Understand Self-Employment Taxes: Pay both the employee's and employer's share of Social Security and Medicare taxes.
- Make Quarterly Payments: Mark your calendar for quarterly estimated tax payments to avoid penalties.
- Track Expenses: Use apps or maintain logs to track income and deductible expenses meticulously.
- Report All Income: Ensure that all gig income is reported accurately, even if you don't receive a 1099 form.
- Set Aside Funds: Regularly set aside a portion of your income for tax payments to avoid year-end surprises.

5. Scholarships, Grants, and Taxes: Keeping It Straight

- Use Funds Appropriately: Understand that funds used for tuition and required supplies are non-taxable, while other uses may be taxable.
- Report Extra Income: Include any taxable portion of scholarships or grants in your income when filing taxes.
- Plan for Tax Implications: Keep detailed records and consider how scholarship funds impact your eligibility for other tax credits and deductions.

Additional Tips

- **Stay Organized**: Regularly update your records and documents to make tax time easier.
- **Consult Professionals**: Seek advice from tax professionals when dealing with complex tax situations.
- **Re-evaluate Periodically**: Review your tax situation periodically, especially after major life changes.

CHAPTER 8
PRACTICAL FINANCIAL PLANNING

" Financial freedom is available to those who learn about it and work for it.

ROBERT KIYOSAKI

Imagine that you're embarking on a road trip. You've got your snacks, playlist, and a vague notion that you're heading somewhere awesome. Wouldn't having a map, a clearly defined route, and some landmarks to visit along the way be better? That's what crafting a personalized financial roadmap is like. It's plotting your course in the financial universe, ensuring that each choice propels you toward your own version of success—be it buying your first car, owning a home, or maybe just ensuring that you can afford to be the life of the party without going broke.

8.1 CREATING A CUSTOMIZED FINANCIAL ROADMAP

Personalized Planning: Crafting Your Financial Future

Let's start with personalizing your financial plan. There isn't a cookie-cutter strategy that works for everyone. Aligning your financial strategy with your personal dreams, circumstances, and the quirky goals that make you, well, you, means your plan won't be the same as your peers. First, define what success looks like on your terms. Is it financial independence by 30? A tech startup? A travel fund that lets you explore the world? Once you have your goals in sight, you can set the GPS coordinates to your desired destination.

Now, think about your resources and limitations. Just as you can't drive a vintage scooter on a freeway at 100 mph, you need to assess your financial vehicle realistically. What's your income? What are your essential expenses? Understanding these helps you figure out how much fuel (read: money) you can divert toward your goals each month. Remember that this plan isn't static; it's a living document. Just as you might suddenly decide to detour to a cool, unplanned destination on a road trip, your financial plan should have the flexibility to adapt to life's unexpected turns.

Milestone Setting: Marking Your Financial Journey

Setting milestones within your financial roadmap is like planting flags on a mountain climb. Each flag marks a significant achievement, giving you a moment to celebrate and reassess. Let's say your goal is to save for a down payment on a house. Break this into smaller milestones. Your first milestone could be saving $1,000, then $5,000, and so on. These milestones keep you motivated and give you clear checkpoints to review your progress.

Adjusting Your Plan: Staying Agile on Your Financial Journey

John Lennon was onto something when he put this old saying into his lyrics, "Life is what happens when you're busy making other plans," the same goes for your financial roadmap. Maybe you land a higher-paying job, decide to go back to school, or face an unexpected financial hurdle. Your financial plan needs to be adjustable to accommodate these changes. Regular check-ins, like a yearly review or a sit-down every time a major life event happens, can help you tweak your roadmap. Maybe you divert more into savings because you've gotten a raise, or perhaps you scale back on investments to fund a return to college. The key is to keep your plan in sync with your life.

8.2 INSURANCE BASICS: WHAT YOU NEED AND WHY

Let's talk about insurance, but let's make it less yawn-inducing. Think of insurance like a trusty umbrella. You might not need it every day, but when an unexpected storm hits—like a sudden downpour of medical bills or car repairs—it's incredibly useful to have around. Most young adults can stay on their parent's insurance until they are 26 or out of college, but there will come a day when you will be on your own and need to take care of insurance like a real adult. Understanding insurance means recognizing that paying monthly premiums creates a safety net, allowing you to sleep soundly at night, secure in the knowledge that life's little (or big) surprises won't wipe you out financially.

Understanding the importance of insurance is like recognizing why you need to charge your phone—without power, it's just a fancy paperweight. Similarly, without insurance, you're one major accident or health issue away from a potential financial disaster. Insurance acts as a financial cushion, absorbing the impact of unexpected costs so you don't have to. By paying premiums, you transfer the risk of significant financial loss to the insurance company, which agrees to cover expenses for various surprise events, such as car accidents, theft, or medical emergencies.

Types of Insurance: Decoding What You Actually Need

Diving into the types of insurance is like walking into a buffet. There's a lot on offer, and while everything might look appealing, you need to pick what best suits your appetite—or, in this case, your needs. The big ones on the menu are health, auto, and renter's insurance. Health insurance is the broccoli of the insurance world—maybe not always exciting, but incredibly good for you. It covers your medical expenses, from doctor's visits to surgeries, and can help you manage the costs of both routine healthcare and unexpected medical issues. Without it, a single health emergency can become a financial disaster.

Then there's auto insurance, which is pretty much mandatory if you drive. It's your car's shield against the slings and arrows of outrageous fortune, like fender-benders or more serious accidents. It covers repairs to your vehicle and protects you against liability if you're at fault in an accident that causes injury or property damage to others.

Renter's insurance, on the other hand, might not be mandatory, but it's no less important, especially if you're fond of your electronics and belongings. It's a security blanket for your stuff. If your rental home is broken into, or if there's a fire or water damage, renter's insurance can help replace your belongings. Plus, it often includes liability coverage, which can be a lifesaver if someone is injured in your rental and decides to sue.

Shopping for Insurance: Finding the Best Fit Without Breaking the Bank

Shopping for insurance can be as tricky as online dating—what looks great at a quick glance might not be the perfect match for you. Comparing policies is key. Don't just look at the premiums; consider what's covered. A cheaper policy might save you money now but could cost you big time if it doesn't cover what you need when disaster strikes. Use online comparison tools to get a range of quotes, and read the fine print. Yes, it's tedious, but understanding exactly what you're covered for—and what you're not—can prevent a world of financial pain later on.

Also, check out reviews and ratings for insurance companies. How do they handle claims? Are customers satisfied with their service? An insurer's responsiveness and support when you're filing a claim can make a huge difference in your experience. It's like choosing a teammate; you want someone reliable who will have your back in a tight spot.

Common Insurance Mistakes to Avoid: Sidestepping Potential Pitfalls

When it comes to insurance, some common blunders can end up costing you. Underinsuring is a classic—like buying rain boots that don't fit. Sure, you saved some money, but you'll get soaked when the storm hits. Always ensure your coverage limits are high enough to fully cover potential losses. On the flip side, there's over-insuring, which is like paying for a gourmet meal you'll never eat. Why shell out for coverage you realistically won't need?

Another frequent error is ignoring deductibles—the amount you pay out of pocket before your insurance kicks in. Opting for a low deductible might seem like a great idea until you see the higher monthly premiums. Sometimes, choosing a higher deductible makes sense if it significantly lowers your premiums and if you have enough savings to cover the deductible in an emergency.

Insurance and Risk Management: Fortifying Your Financial Fortress

In the grand scheme of things, having the right insurance policies is a critical part of managing financial risk. It's knowing your weak spots and fortifying them. Whether the situation is a medical issue, a car accident, or a burglar making off with your laptop, the right insurance can help keep an unfortunate incident from turning into a financial catastrophe. It allows you to plan for the unexpected, providing a safety net that lets you pursue your life and goals with one less worry hanging over your head.

As you navigate the complexities of adulting, give insurance its due consideration. It might not be the most thrilling part of your financial plan, but when life inevitably throws a curveball your way, you'll be glad you have that safety net ready and waiting. Just as a reliable tool is always ready when you need it, your insurance stands by quietly, ready to support you in times of need.

8.3 PLANNING FOR BIG PURCHASES: CARS, COLLEGE, AND MORE

Some of the most exciting chapters of your life involve hefty price tags—like buying your first car, venturing through college, or stepping into a home you can call your own. While these purchases can jazz up your life's soundtrack, they require more than just a spontaneous shopping spree.

Saving Strategies: Building Your Big-Purchase War Chest

First, let's talk about saving strategies. Big-ticket items aren't your everyday purchases; they're more like the boss levels in video games that require extra prep and strategy. Setting aside money for these big purchases should start as early as possible. This is where your savings snowball comes into play—you start small, but as it rolls down the hill, it picks up more snow, growing bigger, faster, and faster. Automate your savings if you can. Set up a separate savings account specifically for your goal, and funnel a portion of your income directly into it. This way, you're not tempted to spend what you can't see.

Consider high-yield savings accounts or certificates of deposit (CDs) for these goals. They offer higher interest rates, meaning your money grows faster without additional effort. If you're saving for something more than five years away, like a down payment on a house, you might even invest some of that money in low-risk bonds or mutual funds. The higher returns can significantly speed up your savings timeline, but remember that greater potential returns come with greater risk, so balance wisely.

Financing Options: Navigating the Seas of Loans and Payment Plans

Unless you've been secretly minting gold in your backyard, chances are you'll need some financing to help cover the costs of things like cars or college tuition. Here's where things can get tricky. Loans and payment plans are double-edged swords—they can cut through financial barriers, making your goals more accessible, but if handled carelessly, they can also hurt your financial health.

When considering loans, whether it's a student loan, mortgage, or car loan, scrutinize the terms. Look at the interest rates, repayment periods, and any penalties for early repayment. Fixed interest rates can offer predictability, preventing nasty surprises if rates go up in the future. However, if you anticipate that you might be able to pay off your debt early, make sure your loan doesn't have prepayment penalties that could eat into what you save on interest.

For college, explore federal student loans first, as they often have more favorable terms and repayment options compared to private loans. For cars and homes, good credit can be your best friend. It can snag you lower interest rates, significantly affecting how much you pay over time. Don't hesitate to shop around and negotiate terms. Sometimes, the sticker price isn't the final price, and this applies to loan conditions as well.

The Impact of Big Purchases on Financial Health: Keeping Your Balance

Big purchases can make or break your financial health. They're like adding heavy weights to your side of the financial seesaw. If not balanced correctly with the rest of your budget, they can leave you teetering on the edge of financial instability. Understanding how a big purchase fits into your overall financial picture is crucial. Will taking on a car payment mean you can't contribute to your retirement for a while? Will student loan repayments delay other financial goals, like buying a home? Mapping out your cash flow with these big purchases in mind can help you see where you might need to adjust your spending or increase your income to keep everything in harmony.

Practical Tips and Considerations: Mastering the Art of Big Purchases

Here are some practical tips. Research is your best tool when planning for a big purchase. Understand the market, know the average costs, and arm yourself with knowledge. For cars, know the best times to buy, like holiday sales, when dealerships are more likely to offer discounts. For homes, understand the local real estate market trends. Are home prices in your area going up or down? Is it a buyer's or a seller's market? For college, consider the return on investment of your chosen field of study. Will your expected future income justify the cost of your education?

Negotiating is another skill to hone. Whether it's the price of the car, the terms of a loan, or even financial aid for college, don't accept the first offer. Be polite, but be persistent. Often, there's room to maneuver that can work to your advantage.

Big purchases are more than just transactions. They're significant financial events that can have long-lasting impacts on your economic landscape. Like any major life decision, they require thought, planning, and a bit of savvy maneuvering. With the right strategies, you can ensure that these purchases enhance your life without derailing your financial goals.

As we wrap up this exploration into planning for big purchases, remember that each decision you make—from the savings plan you choose to the financing options you utilize to the negotiation strategies you employ—plays a crucial role in shaping your financial journey. These aren't just purchases; they're stepping stones to your future. Up next, we'll dive into the world of advanced investment strategies, where we'll explore how to further grow your wealth and secure your financial independence. Stay tuned because the path to financial mastery is just getting started.

ACTION STEPS FOR PRACTICAL FINANCIAL PLANNING

1. Creating a Customized Financial Roadmap

- Define Success: Identify your personal financial goals (e.g., financial independence, startup, travel fund).
- Assess Resources: Determine your income and essential expenses to understand your financial capacity.
- Set Milestones: Break down big goals into smaller, achievable targets (e.g., saving $1,000, then $5,000).
- Regular Reviews: Conduct periodic reviews to adjust your financial plan based on life changes or unexpected events.

2. Insurance Basics: What You Need and Why

- Understand Insurance Types: Know the essential kinds of insurance (health, auto, renter's) and their purposes.
- Shop Smart: Compare insurance policies, not just on premiums, but also on coverage and customer service.
- Avoid Common Mistakes: Ensure adequate coverage without over-insuring, and understand your deductible options.

3. Planning for Big Purchases: Cars, College, and More

- Start Saving Early: Set up separate savings accounts and automate deposits for big purchases.
- Consider High-Yield Accounts: Use high-yield savings accounts or CDs for faster growth of your savings.
- Evaluate Financing Options: Understand loan terms, interest rates, and repayment conditions before committing.

- Research and Negotiate: Thoroughly research the market and negotiate the best deals for your purchases.
- Impact on Financial Health: Assess how big purchases affect your overall financial situation and make necessary adjustments to maintain balance.

CHAPTER 9
PROTECTING YOUR FINANCIAL FUTURE

" *The best way to predict your future is to create it.*

ABRAHAM LINCOLN

Picture this: you're on a roller coaster, strapped in, and about to plunge into a dizzying drop. Your heart races, your palms sweat, and a cocktail of excitement and fear bubbles up—it's thrilling, yet slightly terrifying. Now, imagine if your financial life felt like that all the time. Not so fun, right? That's what unchecked financial anxiety can do to you. It can turn your everyday money management into an emotional roller coaster that leaves you feeling drained. Let's talk about taming that ride, shall we?

9.1 NURTURING YOUR FINANCIAL MENTAL HEALTH

Understanding Financial Anxiety: Unmasking the Hidden Culprit

Financial anxiety sneaks up like a shadow, often disguising itself as fleeting worries about bills or distant thoughts of savings and retirement. But when it takes hold, it morphs into a constant presence, coloring your decisions and potentially leading to sleepless nights staring at the ceiling. What fuels this persistent worry? Often, it's the feeling of uncertainty or a sense of not being in control of your financial destiny. It's like walking through a maze blindfolded, where every turn feels uncertain and fraught with potential pitfalls.

The roots of financial anxiety can often be traced back to early experiences with money. Maybe you saw your parents arguing about bills, or perhaps you experienced financial hardship firsthand. As you take on more financial responsibilities, these moments can plant seeds of worry that grow into gnarly vines of anxiety. The good news? Just as these patterns are learned, they can also be unlearned or managed with the right strategies.

Developing Coping Mechanisms: Tools to Tame the Beast

When financial worries start knocking, don't let them set up camp. One of the first tools in your stress-busting toolkit should be mindfulness. It's not just for yogis or meditation enthusiasts; it's a practical tool for anyone. Mindfulness involves staying present and engaged in the moment rather than letting your mind catastrophize about future financial woes. Try this: the next time you catch yourself spiraling into worry, pause. Breathe deeply, focus on the sensations around you, and gently guide your thoughts back to the present. This practice can help break the cycle of anxiety, providing a mental reset button that keeps financial stress from overwhelming you.

Another powerful tool is proactive financial planning. This doesn't mean you need a spreadsheet for every dollar (unless that's your jam). Rather, you need to establish a clear plan for your income and expenses. Use budgeting apps or spreadsheets or simply write it down on paper—whatever works to give you a clear picture of where your money is going. This clarity can be incredibly soothing to a worried mind, as it replaces uncertainty with structure and predictability.

Setting Realistic Financial Goals: Your Anxiety-Reducing Compass

Setting wildly ambitious financial goals can be as stressful as an over-packed weekend itinerary. There's a place for ambition, but your everyday financial goals should be more like a leisurely stroll than a sprint. Start small. Maybe your first goal is to track your spending for a month or save a small emergency fund of $500. Achieving these smaller goals can provide a sense of accomplishment and build your confidence, making larger goals feel more attainable.

Tailoring your goals to your current life phase and capacity is also crucial. If you're a student or early in your career, your focus might be on slowly building savings or managing student loans rather than investing heavily or buying property. Aligning your goals with your real-life circumstances can prevent feelings of frustration and inadequacy, which are often at the heart of financial anxiety.

Seeking Professional Help: When to Call in the Reinforcements

Just as you'd consult a doctor for a persistent cough, sometimes you need a professional to manage financial stress. How do you know when it's time to seek help? Here's a rule of thumb: if financial worries are keeping you up at night, affecting your relationships, or leading to physical symptoms like headaches or stomach issues, it might be time to talk to a professional. This could be a financial advisor who can help you create a more effective financial plan or a therapist who specializes in financial stress. Remember that seeking help is not a sign of weakness but a proactive step toward regaining your financial peace of mind.

Financial health, much like physical or emotional health, requires attention and care. By understanding the roots of financial anxiety, employing practical coping mechanisms, setting realistic goals, and knowing when to seek professional help, you can protect your financial future and keep your mental health in check. Just like that roller coaster, with the right strategies, you can ensure that your financial life has more ups than downs and that you enjoy the ride a whole lot more.

9.2 STAYING SAFE IN THE DIGITAL FINANCE WORLD

Imagine that you're navigating a bustling digital cityscape—neon signs flashing credit card deals, pop-up ads offering the latest investment tips, and sleek apps that promise the world with just a swipe. Welcome to the digital finance frontier, a place where managing your money is conveniently at your fingertips, but so are the myriad risks that lurk in the electronic shadows. Here, protecting your financial information isn't just about setting a strong password (although that's a start); it's about equipping yourself with a full arsenal of tools and knowledge to safeguard your digital dollars.

Protecting Your Financial Information Online: Fortifying Your Digital Finances

In today's digital age, safeguarding your financial information is crucial. Here's how you can fortify your digital finances:

1. Secure Your Transactions

- Use secure networks for online purchases and accessing financial accounts
- Avoid public Wi-Fi for sensitive transactions
- Verify website legitimacy before entering payment information
- Look for "https" in URLs (the 's' stands for secure)
- Be cautious of poorly designed websites or those with typos

It's like checking the safety gear before a skydive; you want to make sure everything is legit before you jump.

If the worst happens, and you find yourself scammed, it's not game over. First, take a deep breath—it happens to the best of us. Then, spring into action. Contact your bank or credit card company to report the fraud. They can block your card to prevent further unauthorized transactions and may help recover any lost funds. Next, change your online passwords, especially if you suspect they might have been compromised. Report the scam to organizations like the Federal Trade Commission in the U.S. or other relevant authorities in your country. They can't always get your money back, but they can take action to prevent others from falling victim.

Staying informed is your best defense. Scams evolve constantly, and keeping up-to-date on the latest schemes can help you stay one step ahead. Follow reputable tech blogs, subscribe to cybersecurity newsletters, and participate in community forums. Knowledge is power, and in the digital world, it's also your best protector.

Navigating the digital world's dangers doesn't need to be an impossible mission. Equipped with the right knowledge and tools, you can protect yourself from the majority of online threats. Keep your wits about you, trust your instincts, and remember that if something sounds too good to be true, it probably is.

Cryptocurrency Safety: Securing Your Digital Gold

Cryptocurrencies, the digital gold of the internet era, speak to the tech-savvy treasure hunter in all of us. Whether you're dabbling in Bitcoin, Ethereum, or any other crypto, remember that with great digital power comes great responsibility. Cryptocurrencies are stored in digital wallets, and these wallets can be as vulnerable as your physical wallet if not properly secured. Use digital wallets that allow you to keep control of your keys—a set of cryptographic information that lets you access your currency. Think of these keys as the combination to a safe. Store them somewhere secure, not just on a sticky note by your computer.

Moreover, when trading or mining crypto, use reputable exchanges, and keep an eye out for security features like cold storage options, which store the cryptocurrency offline and safe from potential online breaches. Remember that the value of cryptocurrencies can be as volatile as a ride on the stock market—exciting, sure, but with potential drops that aren't for the faint of heart.

9.3 FINANCIALLY PREPARING FOR LIFE'S UNEXPECTED EVENTS

Let's face it—life loves to throw curveballs. One day, you're sailing smoothly, and the next, you're hit with a job loss or a medical emergency that feels more like a strikeout. It's like playing a game of dodgeball blindfolded—you never know when a ball might come flying in your direction. That's why having a game plan for those "just in case" moments isn't only smart; it's essential for keeping your sanity and your savings intact.

The Importance of Emergency Planning: Why It's Your Financial BFF

Imagine this: you're heading home after your last final of the semester, and then, out of nowhere, your car decides to break down in the middle of nowhere. Panic mode, right? Now, if you had roadside assistance or a spare tire ready, that hiccup wouldn't turn into a holiday horror story. That's what an emergency fund does for your financial life. It prepares you for those unexpected breakdowns along the way, ensuring that they're just pit stops, not the end of the road.

Building an emergency fund isn't about being pessimistic; it's about being realistic. Life is unpredictable, and job security can sometimes feel as stable as a house of cards. A robust emergency fund acts like a financial shock absorber, helping you navigate through life's ups and downs without derailing your long-term financial goals. It's the buffer that keeps you from racking up debt when life decides to spice things up.

Insurance as a Safety Net: Not All Heroes Wear Capes

While your emergency fund is there to catch you when you fall, insurance is there to make sure you don't fall too hard. Health insurance is like your health guardian, stepping in when medical bills threaten. Then there's disability insurance, the protector of your income, ensuring that an accident or illness doesn't derail your financial stability. Let's not forget life insurance, the silent guardian for those you might leave behind, providing financial support in your absence.

Each type of insurance serves a unique role in your financial safety net. Without them, you're essentially walking a tightrope with no safety harness. Not an ideal scenario, right? By transferring significant financial risks to an insurance company, you reduce the burden on your emergency fund and ensure that a bump in the road doesn't turn into a full-blown financial crash.

Creating a Financial Contingency Plan: Your Blueprint for the Unexpected

Now, let's talk about stitching all these pieces together into a comprehensive financial contingency plan. This plan is your blueprint for handling financial emergencies—it outlines what steps to take, who to contact, and which resources to tap into when things go south.

Start by listing all your financial accounts, insurance policies, and emergency contacts. Note the passwords or answers to challenge questions, too. Choose a very safe place to keep all this private information.

Next, communicate your plan. If you have family or a partner, make sure they know where to find this information and understand what to do in case you're unable to manage your finances. It's like rehearsing an emergency drill—you hope you never need it, but you'll feel a heck of a lot better knowing it's there.

Regularly update this plan as your financial situation evolves. Got a new job? Update it. Paid off a loan? Update it. The more current your plan, the more effective it'll be when it's needed. Remember that the goal here isn't to obsess over what could go wrong; it's to feel empowered and ready for whatever comes your way.

By building a robust emergency fund, investing in the right insurance, and crafting a detailed financial contingency plan, you're not just preparing for the unexpected—you're ensuring that whatever life throws at you, you're ready to catch it, deal with it, and move on.

9.4 CONTINUOUS LEARNING IN PERSONAL FINANCE

Think of personal finance as your own blockbuster movie series, where every new release (or phase of your life) comes with different challenges and adventures. Just when you think you've mastered the basics—BOOM!—life throws in a twist, like a new tax regulation, an investment opportunity, or a revolutionary financial app. That's why treating financial education as a one-off event is like walking out of the theater mid-movie; you miss out on how the story evolves. The truth is that the landscape of personal finance is ever-changing, and staying informed is the only way to keep your finances in blockbuster shape.

Why is ongoing education in personal finance so important? It keeps you agile and prepared. Financial norms evolve, new financial products emerge, and economic conditions fluctuate. Each stage of your life will bring new financial decisions—buying a home, investing in stocks, saving for retirement. Continuous learning equips you with the knowledge to make informed decisions and to adapt strategies that fit your evolving needs. It's about staying relevant in the game of money, ensuring you're not making decisions based on outdated rules.

Now, let's talk about resources. The world is teeming with knowledge, and thanks to the internet, much of it is right at your fingertips. For those hungry to deepen their financial understanding, a myriad of books, podcasts, and websites offer great insights. Start with books that tackle broad financial principles or that delve into specific topics like investing or debt management.

Websites like *Investopedia*, *NerdWallet*, or *The Financial Diet* make learning about personal finance approachable and practical. They break down complex topics into digestible articles that cater to beginners and seasoned finance buffs alike. These platforms often update their content to reflect current trends and changes in the financial landscape, helping you stay on top of your financial game without feeling overwhelmed.

Why stop at digital resources? Attending workshops and seminars offers distinct benefits, too. These events provide a dynamic learning environment where you can interact with experts and peers. Whether it's an in-person retirement planning seminar or an online budgeting workshop, these sessions can offer personalized advice and answer specific questions you might have. Plus, they often provide networking opportunities that could lead to mentorships or professional relationships beneficial to your financial journey.

Part of learning is sharing—that's where the real mastery of knowledge comes in. Sharing what you've learned about personal finance with your community not only cements your own understanding but also uplifts those around you. Whether it's explaining the basics of budgeting to a friend or starting a blog about your investment journey, teaching others allows you to refine your knowledge and spot gaps in your understanding. It's a win-win: you reinforce your learning and help others navigate their financial landscapes more confidently.

As we wrap up this chapter, consider continuous learning in personal finance not just as a tool for personal empowerment, but also as a key for fostering a financially literate society. The more you learn and share, the better equipped you become to make sound financial decisions, adapting to the ever-changing economic environment with ease and confidence.

ACTION STEPS FOR PROTECTING YOUR FINANCIAL FUTURE

1. Nurturing Your Financial Mental Health

- Identify Financial Anxiety: Recognize and understand the root causes of your financial worries.
- Practice Mindfulness: Use mindfulness techniques to stay present and manage financial stress.
- Create a Budget: Establish a clear budget to understand and control your income and expenses.
- Set Realistic Goals: Define achievable financial goals that match your current life stage.
- Seek Professional Help: Consult a financial advisor or therapist if financial anxiety significantly impacts your well-being.

2. Staying Safe in the Digital Finance World

- Use Strong Passwords: Ensure that all your financial accounts are protected with strong, unique passwords.
- Enable Two-Factor Authentication: Add an extra layer of security to your accounts.

- Regularly Update Software: Keep your financial apps and software up-to-date to protect against vulnerabilities.
- Be Wary of Phishing: Avoid clicking on suspicious links or sharing personal information online.
- Stay Informed: Keep up with the latest cybersecurity practices and digital finance scams.

3. Financially Preparing for Life's Unexpected Events

- Build an Emergency Fund: Save 3-6 months' worth of living expenses in an accessible account.
- Get Insurance: Ensure that you have adequate health, disability, and life insurance to cover potential risks.
- Create a Contingency Plan: Document your financial accounts, insurance policies, and emergency contacts.
- Communicate Your Plan: Make sure your family understands and can access your contingency plan.
- Review and Update Regularly: Periodically update your contingency plan to reflect any changes in your financial situation.

4. Continuous Learning in Personal Finance

- Read Financial Books: Stay informed by reading books on personal finance and investing.
- Listen to Podcasts: Subscribe to finance-related podcasts to gain insights during your commute or free time.
- Use Online Resources: Regularly visit reputable financial websites for up-to-date information.
- Attend Workshops and Seminars: Participate in events to learn from experts and to network with peers.
- Share Knowledge: Teach others about personal finance to reinforce your understanding and to help your community.

KEEPING THE GAME ALIVE

Now that you have everything you need to master money management, avoid costly mistakes, invest like a pro, and secure your financial future, it's time to pass on your newfound knowledge and show other readers where they can find the same help.

Simply by leaving your honest opinion of this book on Amazon, you'll show other teens and young adults where they can find the information they're looking for. Your review could change their lives forever!

Thank you for your help. Financial literacy is kept alive when we pass on our knowledge – and you're helping us to do just that.

Scan the QR code to leave your review on Amazon

https://amzn.to/472gr69

CONCLUSION: YOUR JOURNEY TO FINANCIAL EMPOWERMENT

As you reach the end of this guide, remember that financial literacy is not a destination, but a continuous journey. You've taken the first significant steps by diving into the essentials of money management, from budgeting and saving to investing and understanding taxes. Each chapter has equipped you with the tools and knowledge needed to navigate the often complex world of finance with confidence and clarity.

Reflect on where you started—perhaps feeling overwhelmed by financial jargon or unsure about making the right money decisions. Now, envision your future self: confident, informed, and ready to take charge of your financial destiny. Whether it's setting up a robust budget, opening your first investment account, or simply understanding your paycheck, every skill you've learned here contributes to building a secure and prosperous future.

Remember that the goal is not just to avoid financial pitfalls but also to thrive financially. Stay curious, keep learning, and adapt as you go. The financial landscape will continue to evolve, but with the foundation you've built through this book, you'll be prepared to handle whatever comes your way. Embrace the journey, continue to seek knowledge, and most importantly, apply what you've learned.

Financial freedom is within your reach. With dedication and the right mindset, you can achieve the financial independence you dream of. Go ahead, take control, and make your financial future as bright and secure as possible. Your journey has just begun, and the possibilities are endless.

REFERENCES

- Financial Literacy for Teens: How to Teach Your Teen. (n.d.). Washington Federal. Retrieved from https://www.wafdbank.com/blog/family-finance/financial-literacy-for-teens
- How to Budget With a Low Income. (n.d.). Ramsey Solutions. Retrieved from https://www.ramseysolutions.com/budgeting/how-to-budget-money-with-low-income
- Introduction to Investing. (n.d.). Investor.gov. Retrieved from https://www.investor.gov/introduction-investing
- 7 Common Banking Fees and How to Avoid Them. (n.d.). Experian. Retrieved from https://www.experian.com/blogs/ask-experian/how-to-avoid-bank-fees/
- The Best Money Apps for Kids and Teens in 2024. (n.d.). Dough Roller. Retrieved from https://www.doughroller.net/best-money-apps-for-kids-and-teens
- 8 Financial Tips for Young Adults. (n.d.). Investopedia. Retrieved from https://www.investopedia.com/articles/younginvestors/08/eight-tips.asp
- How To Save Money In College: 50 Different Ideas To Try. (n.d.). The College Investor. Retrieved from https://thecollegeinvestor.com/22453/save-money-in-college/
- Omololu, E. (2024, March 15). 9 Financial Mistakes To Avoid In Your 20s And 30s. Forbes. Retrieved from https://www.forbes.com/sites/enochomololu/2024/03/15/9-financial-mistakes-to-avoid-in-your-20s-and-30s/
- Emergency Fund Calculator – Forbes Advisor. (n.d.). Forbes. Retrieved from https://www.forbes.com/advisor/banking/emergency-fund-calculator/#:~:
- High-yield savings account vs. traditional savings account: Which is better? (n.d.). Yahoo Finance. Retrieved from https://finance.yahoo.com/personal-finance/high-yield-savings-account-vs-traditional-savings-account-which-is-better-120024972.html
- Washington Federal. (n.d.). Financial literacy for teens: How to teach your teen. Retrieved from https://www.wafdbank.com/blog/family-finance/financial-literacy-for-teens
- Ramsey Solutions. (n.d.). How to budget with a low income. Retrieved from https://www.ramseysolutions.com/budgeting/how-to-budget-money-with-low-income

- Investor.gov. (n.d.). Introduction to investing. Retrieved from https://www.investor.gov/introduction-investing
- Experian. (n.d.). 7 common banking fees and how to avoid them. Retrieved from https://www.experian.com/blogs/ask-experian/how-to-avoid-bank-fees/
- Dough Roller. (n.d.). The best money apps for kids and teens in 2024. Retrieved from https://www.doughroller.net/best-money-apps-for-kids-and-teens
- Investopedia. (n.d.). 8 financial tips for young adults. Retrieved from https://www.investopedia.com/articles/younginvestors/08/eight-tips.asp
- The College Investor. (n.d.). How to save money in college: 50 different ideas to try. Retrieved from https://thecollegeinvestor.com/22453/save-money-in-college/
- Omololu, E. (2024, March 15). 9 financial mistakes to avoid in your 20s and 30s. Forbes. Retrieved from https://www.forbes.com/sites/enochomololu/2024/03/15/9-financial-mistakes-to-avoid-in-your-20s-and-30s/
- Forbes. (n.d.). Emergency fund calculator – Forbes advisor. Retrieved from https://www.forbes.com/advisor/banking/emergency-fund-calculator/#:
- Yahoo Finance. (n.d.). High-yield savings account vs. traditional savings account: Which is better? Retrieved from https://finance.yahoo.com/personal-finance/high-yield-savings-account-vs-traditional-savings-account-which-is-better-120024972.html
- FlexJobs. (n.d.). The gig economy: Definition, pros & cons, and finding jobs. Retrieved from https://www.flexjobs.com/blog/post/what-is-the-gig-economy-v2/
- Upwork. (n.d.). How to become a freelancer in 2024: The complete guide. Retrieved from https://www.upwork.com/resources/how-to-become-a-freelancer
- Investopedia. (n.d.). 10 successful young entrepreneurs. Retrieved from https://www.investopedia.com/10-successful-young-entrepreneurs-4773310
- Internal Revenue Service. (n.d.). How to file your taxes: Step by step. Retrieved from https://www.irs.gov/how-to-file-your-taxes-step-by-step
- Internal Revenue Service. (n.d.). Credits and deductions for individuals. Retrieved from https://www.irs.gov/credits-and-deductions-for-individuals
- Internal Revenue Service. (n.d.). Gig economy tax center. Retrieved from https://www.irs.gov/businesses/gig-economy-tax-center
- TurboTax. (n.d.). Taxes for grads: Do scholarships count as taxable income? Retrieved from https://turbotax.intuit.com/tax-tips/college-and-

education/taxes-for-grads-do-scholarships-count-as-taxable-income/
L2hWn0lpe#:~

- Discover. (n.d.). How to create a financial vision board. Retrieved from
  https://www.discover.com/online-banking/banking-topics/financial-
  vision-board/

- Investopedia. (n.d.). Insurance: Definition, how it works, and main types
  of insurance. Retrieved from https://www.investopedia.com/terms/i/
  insurance.asp

- Edward Jones. (n.d.). How to save money for big purchases. Retrieved
  from https://www.edwardjones.com/us-en/market-news-insights/
  investor-education/investment-age/big-purchases

- TheStreet. (n.d.). Why you need a financial roadmap and how to build
  one. Retrieved from https://www.thestreet.com/retirement-daily/your-
  money/why-you-need-a-financial-roadmap-and-how-to-build-one

- Wise. (n.d.). The 9 best online banks in 2023. Retrieved from https://wise.
  com/us/blog/best-online-bank

- NerdWallet. (n.d.). Best investing apps of May 2024. Retrieved from
  https://www.nerdwallet.com/best/investing/investment-apps

- CNBC Select. (n.d.). 5 tips on what to look for when choosing a
  budgeting app. Retrieved from https://www.cnbc.com/select/what-to-
  look-for-in-budgeting-app/

- Federal Deposit Insurance Corporation. (2021, October). Avoiding scams
  and scammers. Retrieved from https://www.fdic.gov/resources/
  consumers/consumer-news/2021-10.html

- HelpGuide. (n.d.). Coping with financial stress. Retrieved from https://
  www.helpguide.org/articles/stress/coping-with-financial-stress.htm

- U.S. Bank. (n.d.). Mindset matters: How to practice mindful spending.
  Retrieved from https://www.usbank.com/financialiq/manage-your-
  household/personal-finance/how-to-practice-mindful-spending.html

- Investors Cabin. (n.d.). The impact of social media on teen spending
  habits. Retrieved from https://investorscabin.com/articles/the-impact-of-
  social-media-on-teen-spending-habits

- Consumer Financial Protection Bureau. (n.d.). An essential guide to
  building an emergency fund. Retrieved from https://www.
  consumerfinance.gov/an-essential-guide-to-building-an-emergency-fund/

- Annuity.org. (n.d.). Financial literacy statistics. Retrieved from
  https://www.annuity.org/financial-literacy/financial-literacy-statistics

- Berger, R. (n.d.). Round up apps. Retrieved from https://robberg-
  er.com/round-up-apps

- Consumer Financial Protection Bureau. (n.d.). An essential guide to
  building an emergency fund. Retrieved from https://www.consumerfi-
  nance.gov/an-essential-guide-to-building-an-emergency-fund/

- Protective. (n.d.). What freelancers need to know about taxes in the gig economy. Retrieved from https://www.protective.com/learn/what-freelancers-need-to-know-about-taxes-in-the-gig-economy
- LegalZoom. (n.d.). Commonly missed tax deductions for gig workers. Retrieved from https://www.legalzoom.com/articles/commonly-missed-tax-deductions-for-gig-workers
- Investopedia. (n.d.). One thing gig workers need to know about tax liability. Retrieved from https://www.investopedia.com/fa-one-thing-gig-worker-tax-liability-8621932
- TurboTax. (n.d.). Side giggers: Tax tips for side jobs. Retrieved from https://turbotax.intuit.com/tax-tips/self-employment-taxes/side-giggers-tax-tips-for-side-jobs/L602518Uh
- Super Lawyers. (n.d.). How to do your taxes in the gig economy. Retrieved from https://www.superlawyers.com/resources/tax/new-york/how-to-do-your-taxes-in-the-gig-economy/

www.ingramcontent.com/pod-product-compliance
Lightning Source LLC
Chambersburg PA
CBHW071651210326
41597CB00017B/2177